Thutmose IV as the Exodus Pharaoh:

Chronological and Astronomical Considerations

Wayne A. Mitchell and David F. Lappin

Thutmose IV as the Exodus Pharaoh: Chronological and Astronomical Considerations

ISBN: 978-1-969368-84-4

Front cover: State chariot of Pharaoh Thutmose IV from Tomb KV 43, displayed at National Museum of Egyptian Civilization in Cairo. The photo by Richard Mortel was cropped, Wikimedia Commons CC-by-2.0. Back cover: (Above) Reconstruction of the palaces near the Nile River at Avaris, © Manfred Bietak. Reproduced by permission. (Below) Moses-Nile image courtesy of gospelimages.com.

Contents

Tables

Figures

Abbreviations

AAA	Annals of Archaeology and Anthropology
AcAr	Acta Archaeologica
AeAT	Ägypten und Altes Testament
AEundL	Ägypten und Levante/Egypt and the Levant
AOF	Altorientalische Forschungen
APA	Acta Praehistorica et Archaeologica
ASV	American Standard Version of the Bible
AulaOr	Aula Orientalis
BAR	Biblical Archaeology Review
BASOR	Bulletin of the American Schools of Oriental Research
B&S	Bible & Spade
BiOr	Bibliotheca Orientalis
BJS	Brown Judaic Studies
BRB	Biblical Research Bulletin
BSFE	Bulletin de la Société française d'Égyptologie
BW	The Biblical World
ca.	circa
CdE	Chronique d'Egypte
cent.	century
cf.	compare
CG	Catalogue Général
Chr	Chronicles
comm.	communication
CSB	Christian Standard Bible
DE	Discussions in Egyptology
Deut	Deuteronomy
EA	El Amarna Letter
e.g.	for example
ESV	English Standard Version of the Bible
Et	Études et Travaux
et al.	and others
Exod	Exodus

Ezek	Ezekiel
Gen	Genesis
GM	Göttinger Miszellen
GTJ	Grace Theological Journal
Heb	Hebrews
Herit Sci	Heritage Science
ICC	Proceedings of the International Conference on Creationism
IES	Israel Exploration Society
IJHCS	International Journal of History and Cultural Studies
JAEI	Journal of Ancient Egyptian Interconnections
JAMT	The Journal of Archaeological Method and Theory
JAOS	Journal of the American Oriental Society
JARCE	Journal of the American Research Center in Egypt
JdE	Journal d'Entrée Inventory Number
JEH	Journal of Egyptian History
JoC	Journal of Creation
JETS	Journal of the Evangelical Theological Society
JNES	Journal of Near Eastern Studies
Josh	Joshua
JRAS	Journal of the Royal Asiatic Society
JSQ	Jewish Studies Quarterly
JSSEA	The Journal of the Society for the Study of Egyptian Antiquities
KBo	Keilschrifttexte aus Boghazköi
Kgs	Kings
KJV	King James Version of the Bible
KUB	Keilschrifturkunden aus Boghazköi
LB	Late Bronze Age
Lev	Leviticus
LSS	Let the Stones Speak
LXX	Greek Translation of the Old Testament
MJTHR	Minia Journal of Tourism and Hospitality Research

Mss	Manuscripts
MT	Masoretic Text, Hebrew and Aramaic
n.	note
NAB	New American Bible
NCV	New Century Version of the Bible
NEAS	Near East Archaeological Society
NIV	New International Version of the Bible
NJPS	New Jewish Publication Society Old Testament
NRSV	New Revised Standard Version of the Bible
Num	Numbers
OINN	Oriental Institute News & Notes
PEQ	Palestine Exploration Quarterly
Per.	Personal
Ps	Psalms
SAK	Studien zur Altägyptischen Kultur
SAOC	Studies in Ancient Oriental Civilization
TMSJ	The Masters Seminary Journal
TT	Theban Tomb
VAT	Vorderasiatisches Museum, Berlin
Vg	Latin Vulgate Version of the Bible
viz.	namely
VT	Vetus Testamentum
YES	Yale Egyptological Studies
ZÄS	Zeitschrift für Ägyptische Sprache und Altertumskunde

Thutmose IV as the Exodus Pharaoh: Chronological and Astronomical Considerations

Wayne A. Mitchell and David F. Lappin

Abstract: It has been proposed from historical synchronisms that Thutmose IV was the Pharaoh of the Exodus. Previous chronological studies suggest that the Exodus occurred in 1446 BC. These hypotheses were tested with astronomical evidence (lunar, solar, and Sothic), historical records, and archaeology.

Introduction

Egyptian chronology of the second millennium BC is essential for the Levant, Syria, Mesopotamia, and the Aegean. Several chronologies are bound to the absolute dating of Ramesses II, based on a single lunar date (Gautschy 2014: 141), and the Low Chronology accession date of 1279 BC for Ramesses II based on the lunar date "is by no means certain" (Huber 2011: 172). For the 18th to 19th Egyptian Dynasties, high and low chronologies have had a level of uncertainty of about 25 years, and chronologies formulated by scholars can yield differences of fifty years or so from the highest to the lowest (Kitchen 1996: 1–13).

One method of investigation involves alignment of historical event patterns. Using this methodology from biblical and Egyptian materials, Collins (2005: 49) located alignments which suggest that "only an Exodus

1

contemporaneous with the end of the reign of Tuthmosis [or Thutmose] IV provides an adequate context for the predicted impacts of the Exodus core events upon Egypt."

Date of the Exodus

To test this hypothesis requires a comparison and then a concatenation of relevant information that dates the Exodus. 1 Kgs 6:1 (MT, LXX(L), Aquila, Symmachus, Vg)[1] states lit., "In the 80th year and 400th year of the going-out of the descendants of Israel from the land of Egypt, in the 4th year of Solomon's reign over Israel, in the month Ziv, which is the 2nd month, he began to build the temple of YHWH." The span of time from the 4th of Solomon in the second month of Ziv/Iyyar to the 15th of the 1st month of Abib/Nisan at the Exodus is therefore 479 years plus between 15 and 45 days (Wood 2008a: 100; cf. Whiston and Tooke 1702: 75; Finegan 1964: 162–163; McFall 2010: 483 n. 16; Steinmann 2011: 46). The notion by those of the late-date Exodus/Conquest (13th cent. BC) Model that the writer of 1 Kgs 6:1 provided a schematic number based on 12 x 40 (e.g., Curtis 1889: 399), is therefore untenable.

A variant for 1 Kgs 6:1 is 440th or 439 years (LXX(BA)). DeVries (1985: 87 n. 1a; Cogan 2001: 236; Smith 2024: 59) concludes that this variant is revisionistic, though a copyist parablepsis in an early square script to the word for the number 40 two words later in the Hebrew *Vorlage* is also possible.

---

[1] Cf. Smith (2024: 41–64).

H. H. Rowley (1950: 10 n. 4) wrote that between AD 1911 and 1945 calculations for the accession of Solomon ranged from 976 BC to 952 BC. Coucke (1928: 1447–1451) appears to be the first to correctly calculate that Solomon's accession began in Tishri 971 BC, his 4th year was Tishri of 968 BC to Tishri 967 BC, and that his last year began in Tishri 932 BC.[2] He concluded that the start of the construction of the Temple was in May/June (Ziv/Iyyar) of 967 BC. These dates have been verified by Young (2003: 602; cf. McFall 2010: 483; Steinmann 2011: 37–41, 133–134). The date of the Exodus was therefore 967 BC + 479 = 1446 BC.

This Exodus date is also supported by Judg 11:26, which states that Israel had occupied Heshbon, Aroer, the surrounding settlements, and all the towns along the Arnon river for 300 years at the time of Jephthah. With ca. 1100 BC[3] for Jephthah, ca. 1100 BC + 300 = ca. 1400 BC + 40 years wilderness sojourn = ca. 1440 BC.

1 Chr 6:33–37 presents 18 generations from Korah (Num 16; cf. Exod 6:16–21) in Moses' time to Heman (1 Chr 6:31; 15:16–17) in David's time. An addition of a generation

---

[2] Young demonstrated that Solomon died between Tishri 1 of 932 BC and Tishri 1 of 931 BC. Thiele (1983) assumed that Solomon died in the latter half of 931 BC, between Tishri 931 BC and the end of Adar 930 BC, and this led to a one-year discrepancy in his chronology. The correction moves the starting year for Ataliah and preceding Judean kings by one year versus Thiele's chronology (Steinmann 2011: 133–134).

[3] Osgood (1984: 158): "1103 BC"; Steinmann (2011: 107): "1088 BC."

brings the chronology to Solomon. With 25 years to a generation (Bright 1972: 113), 19 x 25 = 475 years + 967 BC = ca. 1442 BC, the approximate date of the Exodus (Stripling 2021: 31; Wood 2005: 485–486; cf. Bimson 1978: 96), in agreement with 1 Kgs 6:1.

Information in the Seder Olam and the Babylonian Talmud concerning the Sabbatical and Jubilee years states that Ezekiel's vision began on Rosh Hashanah on the 10th of the month, which occurs only at the start of a Jubilee year (cf. Lev 25:9–10), and this took place in the 14th year after Jerusalem was destroyed, i.e. 574 BC. In S. 'Olam Rabbah and b. 'Arak 12a they state that Ezekiel's vision was at the end of the 17th Jubilee cycle. The 17th Jubilee was due in Tishri of 574 BC. The first Jubilee 16 cycles earlier was Tishri 574 BC + (16 x 49) = Tishri of 1358 BC. The Conquest began in Abib/Nisan, thus, the first year of the cycle began 48 years earlier in Abib/Nisan in 1406 BC (cf. Young 2006: 80). Adding the 40 years of the wilderness sojourn results in 1446 BC for the Exodus.

Thutmose IV Reign Length

The highest attested regnal year for Thutmose IV is year 8 from the Konosso Stela. Manetho, a 3rd cent. BC Egyptian priest and historian wrote *Aegyptiaca* (History of Egypt), extant only in the writings of Josephus and Church fathers. Egyptologists have assumed that Manetho's "Thmosis son of Misphragmuthosis," who reigned for 9 years and 8 months, according to Josephus (9 years according to Africanus and Eusebius), is Thutmose IV, and this reign length has been the current consensus. Bryan (1991) remarks that "the identification [of Thmosis with Thutmose IV] is not positive. The list is confused, and Thmosis is preceded not by Amenophis but by Misphragmuthosis." Raspe (1998: 143; Tetley 2014: 444) writes that "Manetho's king-list of the Eighteenth Dynasty appears garbled beyond recognition in both Josephus' and the Church fathers' rendering."

A wine docket from Deir el-Medineh reads "Year 19; Wine of the estate of Menkheprure [Thutmose IV] from the *mw n* Ptah, from the hand of Hekay" (cf. Helck 1988: 154). Bryan (1991: 6) concludes, "Although one cannot absolutely rule that date out until the hieratic paleography has been judged, the date is almost certainly one of a latter New Kingdom ruler." Aston (2012: 293) remarks, "This may thus indicate a regnal year 19, but the Estate of Tuthmosis [Thutmose] IV is certainly attested long after the death of the king," and notes a wine docket of Year 36 found at Malkata "also refers to wine from the Estate of Tuthmosis [Thutmose] IV."

Bryan (1991: 6) adds that the "estate of Thutmose IV is attested in a number of later 18th and 19th dynasty sources," and concludes (1991: 9; cf. Tetley 2014: 397), "To summarize the evidence of contemporary year dates, Thutmose IV is last known by a year 8 inscription at Konosso." Aston (2012: 300) has termed the reign length of Thutmose IV an "enigma," partly due to the *Heb sed* inscriptions of the king. The 3rd pylon at Karnak has a text stating a *Heb sed* festival and a renewal of a *Heb sed* jubilee for Thutmose IV (Letellier 1979: 52–71). A temple at Amada also records a renewal of the *Heb sed* for Thutmose IV (Bryan 1991: 199–203). *Heb sed* festivals were celebrated in a king's year 30, and then at 3- or 4-year intervals. Some have dismissed the *Heb sed* inscriptions as "pillar benedictions" or "unfulfilled wishes" (cf. Aston 2012: 301). Bryan (2000: 249) likewise argues that Thutmose IV planned "a celebration of a first jubilee... without waiting for thirty years to elapse, as was certainly the case with Amenhotep II too."

In addition to the *Heb sed* and wine docket evidence, Aston (2012: 302) argues that the "elite tombs, carved in the reign of Tuthmosis IV" are, "in comparison with those cut during the reigns of Amenophis [Amenhotep] II and Amenophis [Amenhotep] III, a surprisingly high number for a reign which only lasted eight to eleven years, at most." At this point of the investigation, however, the consensus view of 8-10 years for the reign of Thutmose IV is here tentatively accepted. With 1446 BC for the Exodus, this suggests a reign for Thutmose IV of ca. 1455-1446 BC, which is about 55 years earlier than the Low Chronology of 1401-1391 BC, and 29 years earlier than the High Chronology of 1425-1417 BC.

Candidate Ramesses II

Exod 1:11 states, "And they [Israelites] built store cities for Pharaoh: Pithom and Ramesses." Josephus, in ca. 95 AD in Contra Apion I 15, wrote that a king named Armeses Miamun (i.e. Ramesses II) reigned for 66 years and two months, and after him was Amenophis. In Contra Apion I 26, he relates that Manetho speaks of an expulsion of a people known as the Hyksos from Egypt that occurred during Amenophis. In 1569, the great Flemish cartographer Mercator (pp. 23, 25–26) wrote, "Armesesmiamum

[Ramesses II] king of Egypt [reigned] 66 years 2 months. This is without doubt the one who sought to oppress the sons of Israel." He then identified his successor, Amenophis, as the Pharaoh of the Exodus. In 1849, Lepsius (pp. 172–176, 292; 1853: 449–450) also concluded that Ramesses Miamun was the Pharaoh of the Oppression, but that his successor was Merneptah (or Merenptah), and he was the Pharaoh of the Exodus. In 1879 (p. 128), Egyptologist Brugsch likewise wrote that "Mineptah [Merneptah] should in all probability be acknowledged as the Pharaoh of the Exodus."

By 1889 Curtis (p. 398) in Dictionary of the Bible wrote, "The Pharaoh of the Oppression, under whom the children of Israel built the treasure cities Pithom and Ramses (Exod 1:11), was Ramses II," and that "The Exodus has usually been assigned (by Brugsch, Ebers, Rawlinson, Sayce, and others) to the reign of Meneptah [Merneptah], or Seti II." However, in 1896, Petrie discovered the Merneptah Stele, with its mention of Israel, an identifiable sociopolitical ethnic entity in Canaan, and this pushed back the Exodus Pharaoh from Merneptah to the reign of Ramesses II (Breasted 1897: 68; Mahler 1901: 60, 65). This 13th cent. BC Exodus theory became known as the late-date Exodus/Conquest theory or model, and became accepted by many Egyptologists and Bible scholars (Steiner 2016: 80).

In most manuscripts of Gen 47:11 the toponym Ramesses is also used for the area of residence in Egypt where the patriarch Jacob and his family lived, reading "in the land of Egypt, in the best of the land, in the land of Ramesses," and therefore is evidence that the toponym Ramesses (also in Exod 1:11, 12:37 and Num 33:3, 5) may be a later scribal update (cf. Wood 2007: 251), possibly performed during the era of the Judges. The Old Latin manuscript OL(E) for Gen 47:11 lacks Ramesses, reading instead "in the land of Egypt, in the best of the land of Gesem [Goshen]." The original reading for Gen 47:11 is not certain, since an LXX manuscript, LXX(D), reads "in the land of Egypt, in the best of the land," which is the shortest reading (although loss by homoioarcton is possible), though one could argue that the addition of Goshen seems necessary in context. It is thought that the toponym may have originally read either Rowaty, Huwara, or Peru-nefer (Wood 2003: 261; Steinmann 2011: 57; Petrovich 2021: 35).

As noted by Wood (2005: 479), the Israelites "were employed as slave laborers to construct the store cities prior to the reign of Ramesses II." Thus, the toponym Ramesses for the store city has no link to Ramesses II. Notably, the assignment of Ramesses II as the Exodus Pharaoh results in the pharaoh surviving the Red Sea/Yam Suph[4] drowning (Wood 2005: 478), and then he would have continued the

---

[4] Red Sea is the later Greek translation. The Hebrew consonantal text can be vocalized as either yam suph or yam soph, where yam means "water/sea/lake." While Exodus 2:3 uses suph as "reeds/rushes," and suph has been suggested to be a cognate of Egyptian *tjufy* "reeds," the Hebrew verbal form of suph usually means "to come to an end" or "to cease." The noun form of soph means "end" or "boundary." Thus, the usual Hebrew meaning would be "sea/lake of/at the end/boundary," with the minority of Hebrew evidence suggesting "sea/lake of rushes/reeds." Reeds are a fresh water plant, which suggests that the yam suph/soph on the shore of Ezion Geber (1 Kgs 9:26) in the Gulf of Eilat/Aqaba should be translated as "sea at the end/boundary" (of Israel; so also LXX). The yam suph/soph of Exodus 10:19 etc. can therefore relate to any boundary or reed sea/lake.

power of Egypt. In fact, Egyptian hegemony was very strong in Canaan during most of Ramesses' reign, but in the book of Joshua, Egyptian troops are never encountered by the Israelites. If the Exodus is placed in the mid-reign of Ramesses II, the Conquest would have begun toward the end of Merneptah's reign, but the Merneptah Stele already included Israel as one of the enemies of Egypt. Placing the Exodus at the last year of Ramesses II results in the Conquest occurring in the reign of Ramesses III, but this pharaoh had campaigns into the Levant as far as Byblos and possibly into Syria. The evidence therefore casts significant doubt for this candidate.

Furthermore, both Merneptah, in his year 5, and Ramesses III, some 30 years later in years 5, 8, and 11, had sufficient military strength to destroy the invasion forces of confederations of Mediterranean peoples (Sandars 1985: 105–137). These confederations are blamed for the destabilization and then destruction of formerly powerful Near Eastern states, including the Mycenean Kingdoms, the Hittite empire, and several coastal cities of the eastern Mediterranean early in the reign of Ramesses III. If these events coincided with the 'Conquest period,' one might assume the Israelites were able to exploit the chaos in the Near East to complete their conquest of Canaan. However, this appears to be contradicted by biblical accounts (see below).

Candidate Amenhotep II

A prevalent candidate for Pharaoh of the Exodus by those holding to the early-date Exodus/Conquest theory (15th century BC) has been Amenhotep II (Haynes 1896: 249, 252; Jack 1925: 166; Caiger 1936: 192; Rea 1961: 14; Aling 1981: 102; Shea 2003: 41–51; Petrovich 2021: 168–195), that began with a conventional Egyptian High Chronology, e.g., 1453-1416 BC, which overlaps the early reign of Amenhotep II with the Exodus date of 1446 BC. Using the High Chronology, Amenhotep II would have survived the Yam Suph event in year 7 or 8 of his 26 or 37-year reign, and with this chronological alignment he then would have resumed significant military activity in the Levant only 7 months later, with an army strong enough to take captive about 100,000 Asiatics, which were taken back to Egypt (Petrovich 2021: 182–183; cf. Kennedy 2020: 57 n. 31).

Eames (2023: 12) rightly remarks, "[A]fter everything the Bible describes surrounding the plagues–the total destruction and humiliation of Egypt, not to mention the destruction of pharaoh's elite chariot force–is it reasonable to believe Amenhotep II, only *months* later, had the means to engage in one of the most successful military campaigns in history?"

After the reign of Amenhotep II, Thutmose IV continued the might of Egypt with at least one major military campaign into the Levant. It is possible that a tomb scene with the Chiefs of Nahrin before Thutmose IV in his kiosk in year 6 recounts this campaign, though other interpretations are conceivable (Bryan 2000: 250). In the biblical texts, however, it is noted that Moses told the Israelites that "the Egyptians you see today you will never see again" (Exod 14:13), and surely this includes Pharaoh as well. This was accomplished when YHWH "shook off Pharaoh and his army in the Yam Suph" (Ps 136:15; cf. Exod 14:17–18) by drowning (Exod 14:28, 30; 15:4).

Exod 14:27 has similar language to Ps 136:15, "Now the Egyptians were trying to escape from it, but YHWH shook off the Egyptians in the midst of the sea." And, "None of them survived" (Exod 14:28). The proponents of Amenhotep II argue that while Egyptians and Pharaoh's army are mentioned as drowning in Exod 14:27–28, the drowning of Pharaoh is not explicitly mentioned in the book of Exodus (Petrovich 2021: 173–175). The effort to limit the evidence to the book of Exodus is curious.

Exod 14:17 states that YHWH "will gain respect through what happens to Pharaoh and all his army, chariots, and horsemen" (FBV). As noted, "not one" from the Egyptian army chasing the Israelites survived (Exod 14:27–28). Irrefutably, Pharaoh is explicitly stated in Ps 136:15 as being with his army when they were "shook off" by YHWH "in the Yam Suph." Collins (2005: 8; cf. Wood 2005: 253–254) contends that "a straightforward reading of the relevant biblical passages supports that the Pharaoh of the Exodus perished along with his troops when the *yam suph* surged over them," and that "the need to propose a string of secondary and tertiary hypotheses in order to have Pharaoh survive the *yam suph* incident severely weakens any such theory."

In further defense of Amenhotep II as a candidate for Exodus Pharaoh, it is claimed that Exod 2:23, 4:19, and Acts 7:23, 30 require that the Pharaoh previous to the Pharaoh of the Exodus to have reigned over 40 years. The 54-year reign of Thutmose III prior to Amenhotep II is said to be additional support (Petrovich: 2021, 168, 209; Stripling 2021: 32–33;

cf. Rea 1961: 11). But as Habermehl (2013: 16; cf. Hoffmeier 2021: 56) notes, "Ex. 4:19 merely states that more than one person had sought Moses' death, without indicating who these people were, and there is nothing to say that the same pharaoh had reigned all that time. We can infer from Ex. 2:23 only that the pharaoh who died was the last of those who wanted Moses dead."

Another assertion put forward by proponents of Amenhotep II is that Manetho believed the Exodus Pharaoh was named Amenophis (Haynes 1896: 249; Jack 1925: 116; Petrovich 2021: 169; Stripling 2021: 32–33; cf. Mercator 1569: 25), and should be identified as Amenhotep II. Josephus (Contra Apion I 26) discusses Manetho's expulsion account, which occurred during a Pharaoh Amenophis, and Manetho tells the same story twice, but with different details. These accounts have been termed Manetho A and B. Apparent variants of the expulsion accounts are found in the writings of Chaeremon, Lysimachus, Apion, Hecataeus of Abdera, Diodorus Siculus, Pompeius Trogus, and Tacitus.

In Manetho A, Josephus identifies the expulsion of the Hyksos with the Jews, but while Manetho says that it was during Amenophis, Josephus says that "Tethmosis" [Thutmose] was king when they "went away." In Manetho B, there is a seer named Amenophis under Pharaoh Amenophis, and the pharaoh has a son named Sethos, also called Ramesses. The people in revolt, to be expelled, appointed a priest from Heliopolis named Osarsiph, who later changed his name to Moses. According to Day (1995: 378), "It is generally agreed that this Pharaoh [Amenophis] is a conflation of Merneptah and Akhenaten (Amenhotep

IV)." Others identify the seer as the royal scribe Amenhotpe under Amenhotep III, with elements apparently derived from the time of Ramesses III. Raspe (1998: 135, 145) concludes that the two expulsion accounts found in Manetho originally had nothing to do with the Jews, but have been tampered with in order to allow for an anti-Jewish interpretation.

Thus, the idea of Amenhotep II as a candidate for Exodus Pharaoh based on a High Chronology, an Exodus at 1446 BC, dubious interpretations of Exod 2:23, 4:19 and Acts 7:23, and late corrupted expulsion stories by Manetho, results in absurd events where hard-hearted Pharaoh alone escapes the Yam Suph incident, while his army, which included "all the chariots of Egypt" (Exod 14:7), does not, and only 7 months after the plague of the firstborn and loss of his army the Pharaoh has an army large enough to undertake a major military campaign into the Levant and take back to Egypt 100,000 captive Asiatics.

It should be mentioned that Amenhotep II, as a candidate for Exodus Pharaoh based on a High Chronology, supported by Manetho's Amenophis, (and Hatshepsut as Pharaoh's daughter), are all theories proposed by Captain A. E. Haynes (p. 249) in his article published in 1896.

While the evidence at this point has shown significant problems for Amenhotep II as a candidate for Exodus Pharaoh, moving his last year to 1446 BC solves several problems. A discussion of the evidence with this adjustment will be presented below.

Candidate Thutmose III

Another candidate for the Exodus Pharaoh has been Thutmose III (e.g., Wilkinson 1878: 2; Shea 1979: 230–238; Finegan 1998: 228). This overlap with 1446 BC occurs using the Low Chronology[5] (1479-1425 BC). Following the Exodus, Thutmose III alone would have survived the Yam Suph event and then would have continued to exert Egyptian hegemony (Hoffmeier 2021: 57). The Conquest of Canaan by the Israelites would have occurred toward the end of Amenhotep II's reign, at a time of significant Egyptian power. The historical records, therefore, make Thutmose III an unlikely candidate.

Deuteronomy 11:4

An additional text to consider is from the book of Deuteronomy, which contains speeches by Moses during a 40-day period in 1406 BC while the Israelites were encamped in the plains of Moab east of the Jordan River. In Deut 11:4, Moses reminds the Israelites what YHWH did "to the army of Egypt, to their horses and to their chariots, how he made the water of the Red Sea flow over them as they pursued you, and how the LORD [YHWH] has destroyed them to this day" (ESV). The Hebrew word abad means "destroyed, devastated, ruined, broken." The word is used in

---

[5] The High Chronology for Thutmose III is 1504-1450 BC, which misses an overlap by 4 years. An Exodus of 1450 BC would require 4th Solomon at 971 BC, which the chronological data does not support.

Exod 10:7 to describe the condition of Egypt after the seventh plague of hail.

For the meaning of the phrase "to this day," Geoghegan (2006: 14; cf. Peterson 2015: 78–86) lists three options that have dominated discussions of the phrase, "1) 'forever'…, 2) any time before the said entry ceased to exist…, or 3) the biblical author's own day." The common translation of Deut 11:4 as represented by the ESV (cf. ASV, KJV, NAB, NRSV) assumes option 3, that the ruin of Egypt following the Yam Suph incident continued at least until the year of the Conquest of Canaan, 40 years later.

Other translations appear to understand the phrase based on option 1, e.g., "the LORD [YHWH] brought lasting ruin on them" (NIV, cf. CSB, NCV, NJPS). Merrill (1994: 207) assumes option 3, and essentially suggests that the Pharaohs after the Exodus would have been unable "to field large armies or undertake major military campaigns until after the period suggested by 'until this very day,' that is, about 1400 B.C." For the translation of Deut 11:4 with option 3 it is therefore of interest to consider what is known about the power of Egypt following the Exodus Pharaoh candidates Amenhotep II and Thutmose IV, as measured by major military activity in the Levant.

In addition to a campaign of Thutmose IV against an uprising east of Edfu in year 8 (Konosso Stela; cf. Bryan 2000: 251), Ahlstrom (1994: 238) writes that "an inscription at Karnak as well as some inscriptions from tombs of two of his officials report that he conquered Babylon, Naharin, Qadesh, Tunip, Takshi (also in the Orontes Valley), and the Shasu people. As well, he is said to be 'the conqueror of the land of Kharu' (Palestine), and to have taken prisoners from Gezer (?). He is also said to have been at Sidon, according to one of the Amarna letters."

Ahlstrom cautions that while "it is probable that Tuthmosis [Thutmose] had been campaigning in Asia… the engraved reports are too much in style with those of his forefathers. The scribes may have copied part of the inscriptions of Tuthmosis III and Amenhotep II." Egyptian inscriptions are prone to exaggeration, and claims of conquest have to be carefully evaluated. It is generally accepted, however, that Thutmose IV had at least one major military campaign into the Levant (e.g., Bryan 2000: 250).

Amenhotep III had a campaign in Nubia in year 5. While the funerary temple of Amenhotep III at Kom el-Hettân has engraved on a wall "Karkemish," and it is quoted like a conquered, submitted city, De Pietri (2016: 9) concludes that "this is a typical and well attested formula of the pharaoh propaganda." Although objects naming Amenhotep III and his queen are ubiquitous in the Levant, Weinstein (1998: 224) writes that "not once during his nearly four decades on the throne did the king have to lead an Egyptian army onto Asiatic soil."

Ahlstrom (1994: 238; Berman 1998: 22) likewise concludes that Thutmose IV "may also have been the last pharaoh of the Eighteenth Dynasty to campaign in Asia," or until Horemheb (Morkot 2010: 106), and Giveon (1969: 54) remarks that the reign of Amenhotep III "heralds a weakening of Egypt's position in the world." Thus, if one interprets Deut 11:4 as requiring at least 40 years when Pharaohs did not undertake major military campaigns into the Levant, then the 38-year reign of Amenhotep III[6] followed by the reign of Akhenaten, is a more probable fit to this expectation than an era beginning with Thutmose IV.

In light of the above, the historical records concerning Amenhotep II and the continuation of Egyptian power with Thutmose IV do not appear to match the biblical descriptions of a Pharaoh that does not survive the Yam Suph event and is followed by a period lacking major Egyptian power, while the placement of Thutmose IV with his last year at 1446 BC[7] followed by Amenhotep III and Akhenaten does. The hypothesis of Collins for the placement of Thutmose IV based on historical alignments was further tested using evidence from archaeology.

Tell el-Dabʿa

In the Egyptian Delta at ancient Avaris,[8] modern Tell el-Dabʿa, thought to be in the district of biblical Goshen (Kitchen 2003: 261; Bietak 2015a: 22; Petrovich 2021: 125),

---

[6] Possibly relevant is the commissioning by Amenhotep III of over six hundred statues of Sekhmet, the goddess of plague and healing. Also, it is expected that the Exodus Pharaoh and those pharaohs immediately following him would know the name of Yahweh (cf. Exod 3:15; 5:1; 6:3). Amenhotep III apparently knew this name, since his Soleb Hieroglyph lists "the land of the Shasu of Yhw." Cf. also Stripling et al. (2023: 16–17).

[7] Concerning the existence of the mummy of Thutmose IV, cf. Collins (2005: 43).

[8] Avaris is the Greek rendering of Egyptian ḥw.t wʿr.t, pronounced Huware or Hawara, meaning "House of the Region." Cf. also Petrovich (2021: 33–135).

Stratum-b/c "Hiatus" marks an abandonment of the site by the Egyptians and the slaves.[9] The workshops of the slaves were abandoned, leaving their work behind (Petrovich 2013: 12). Stratum-b/c is approximately equivalent to the transition at Late Bronze (LB) IA/LB IB, which is ca. 1400 BC in the conventional low Egyptian chronology. Petrovich assigns LB IA to 1485-1446 BC and LB IB to 1446-1400 BC.[10] For Thutmose IV ca. 1455-1446 BC, LB IA would be ca. 1520-1446 BC.

According to Bietak (phasing chart; 2017: 60; Bryan 2000: 234), the abandonment occurred after Amenhotep II. Petrovich (2021: 180, 184; cf. 2013: 16, 22) argues that the Exodus occurred in the early reign of Amenhotep II in year 7, since the High Chronology he has adopted aligns year 7 with 1446 BC, but this alignment is contrary to Bietak's conclusion of the archaeological evidence that the abandonment occurred *after* the reign of Amenhotep II.

In Stratum-b/c Hiatus to immediately following in Stratum-b/3, Bietak (2006: 123–136) found animal burials, the majority being sheep and goats less than a year old, which he believes occurred somewhere between the beginning of the reign of Thutmose IV and before the latter part of the reign of Amenhotep III.[11] Petrovich (2021: 149–164) believes the burials of sheep and goats less than a

---

[9] Petrovich (2021: 215) assigns Stratum-b/c to ca. 1446-1396 BC.

[10] Cf. Moore (2023: 17). However, cf. fn. 25.

[11] Bietak specifies as "1401-1363 BC," according to the Low Chronology.

year old are connected with the Exodus Passover (cf. Exod 12:5).

Petrovich (2013: 14) also states, "From the available evidence, the possibility certainly exists that the abandonment of Avaris transpired while Thutmose IV was sitting on the throne." In addition to evidence noted by Petrovich, Bietak[12] suggests indirect evidence for Thutmose IV at Tell el-Dab'a, "In the workshops attached to Palace F of Tell el-Dab'a there is a whole series of scarabs of kings of the first half of the 18th Dynasty until Amenhotep II. As these scarabs make only sense in a workshop if they have been discarded after removing their attached rings of gold, this would mean that the workshops were still used until Thutmose IV, as it is hardly perceivable that they were discarded when Amenhotep was still alive."

Aston[13] remarks that "only a small part of Tell el-Dab'a has been excavated, so it is quite likely that scarabs/pottery deposits datable to the reign of Tuthmosis [Thutmose] IV will one day appear." It is therefore reasonable to suggest that the Stratum-b/c Hiatus may have begun 8-10 years after Amenhotep II, at the end of the reign of Thutmose IV.

Jericho, Ai and Hazor

The book of Joshua states that Jericho (6:24), Ai (8:28) and Hazor (11:11) were destroyed and set on fire by the Israelites (1406 BC). If the Exodus occurred after either

---

[12] Per. comm. December 2024.

[13] Per. comm. January 2025.

Amenhotep II or Thutmose IV, evidence of destruction and conflagration at some point approximately between LB IA and LB IIA should exist at these three cities. After evidence for the destruction of Jericho City IV(c) during the Middle Bronze (MB) III, ca. 1550 BC, LB pottery has been found on all sides of the tell by every major excavation, which belongs to Late Bronze Age (LBA) City V(a). LB Egyptian scarabs were also found in tombs that conclude with Amenhotep III, which is LB IB/LB IIA. In addition, a cuneiform tablet similar to the 14th century Tell el-Amarna tablets was found by Garstang.

Concerning LB evidence at the tell, Sellin and Watzinger (1913: 123) found LB pottery sherds in an area known as Spring Hill. Garstang (1934: Pl. XXVII – XXXIX) found LB pottery in the area of the Middle Building. Ceramicist Mullins found that Garstang's published bichrome pottery largely dates to LB IIA (Windle 2025a: 33). Kenyon (Kenyon and Holland 1981: 371) found LB pottery sherds in Trenches I and II, and Nigro (2020a: 204; Windle 2025a: 24) found LB evidence on the eastern, southern, and north-western edges of the tell.

Following the destruction of City IV(c), the site was abandoned for about 100 years and was later rebuilt in ca. 1450 BC during the LBA, designated as City V(a). A mudbrick wall about 6 feet wide and 20 feet high was constructed on top of the MB Cyclopean Wall. Kenyon believed the mudbrick wall dated to City IV(c), but Nigro (2023: 605) has redated the mudbrick wall in Kenyon's trenches I (western), II (northern) and III (southern) from MBA to LBA. Thus, the fallen mudbrick wall formerly thought to be MBA City IV(c) actually belongs to LBA City

V(a). Approximately 50-75 years later the City V(a) mudbrick walls collapsed and the city was destroyed with conflagration (Nigro 2021 ASOR Presentation Slide 7; Windle 2025a: 61–64). As Windle (2025a: 65–67) argues, the destruction of City V(a) was likely by the Israelites.

The city of Ai has been identified in excavations at Khirbet el-Maqatir, with abundant Late Bronze I pottery, and much of it showing conflagration at the end of the Late Bronze IB (Stripling 2021: 44–45). Also, an Amenhotep II scarab was found in 2013 under a concentration of ash of a sealed locus dating to Late Bronze I.

At Hazor (Tell el-Qedah), a Late Bronze I destruction layer was found at Stratum XV in the upper city and Stratum 2 in the lower city (Stripling 2021: 45–46). Decapitated figurines from the Late Bronze were also found, and in 2014 at Khirbet el-Maqatir, a decapitated bronze ram's head was found in a Late Bronze context (Moore 2023: 16, 18). In Num 33:52 and Deut 12:2-3, commands are given to destroy pagan idols.

To further test the hypothesis of Collins, astronomical records (Sothic, lunar, solar eclipse, solar alignment) and additional historical records will be utilized to evaluate if such an earlier move of Thutmose IV is possible.

Astronomical Records: Amenhotep I to Amenhotep II

Astronomical records of the New Kingdom include lunar dates (Table 1) and two records of the heliacal rising of Sirius, Sothis to the Greeks. The Ebers papyrus records on two rows a rising of Sirius in year 9 of Amenhotep I with date III *šmw* 9. This is thought to be a heliacal rising of

Sirius. The other Sirius record is from a stone from the remnants of the temple of Khnum on the island of Elephantine.

It has an inscription which states that the feast of the heliacal rising of Sirius was on 28th Epiphi, which equals III *šmw* 28, though the year is missing. The stone is part of a feast list with information apparently from the time of Thutmose III. The locations for the observations of the risings of Sirius are unknown, and the lunar records have several possible solutions.

Pharaoh	Year	Date
Thutmose III	23	I *šmw* 21
Thutmose III	24	II *prt* 30
Amenhotep II	3	III *šmw* 15
Amenhotep II	20	III *šmw* 11
Amenhotep II	21	II *šmw* 30
Amenhotep III	21	III *šmw* 1
Ramesses II	52	II *prt* 27
Twosre	7	II *šmw* 28
Ramesses III	7	III *šmw* 9
Ramesses VI	3	II *šmw* 20
Ramesses VII	6	III *šmw* 9
Ramesses XI	22	II *šmw* 22

Table 1: Lunar data from the Egyptian 18th-20th Dynasties

While there can be many solutions to the lunar records, the observations of the heliacal rising of Sirius have fewer solutions. This situation has led to high, middle, and low chronologies for the New Kingdom. Most Egyptologists favor the Low Chronology (Hoffmeier 2021: 56).

For Amenhotep I, the conventional Low Chronology is based on an observation at Thebes, with a heliacal Sirius rising in year 9 of Amenhotep I in 1517 BC, accession 1526 BC. This is compatible with the accession of Thutmose III in 1479 BC. For the the High Chronology, the observation was at Memphis or Heliopolis, and the heliacal rising of Sirius in 1537 BC, resulting in accession of Amenhotep I 1545 BC. This is compatible with the accession of Thutmose III in 1504 BC. The high and low accession dates for Thutmose III are derived from two lunar dates recorded during his reign. A year 23 record is for the battle of Megiddo on I *šmw* 21 which may be *psḏntyw* or the day after.

The Egyptian term *psḏntyw* refers to an event at the transition from the old to the new lunar month. According to Parker (1950: 9–23; 1957: 39–43), the day of the new moon started at dawn following lunar disappearance[14] (LD) on day 29 or day 30 of a lunar month, and this has been used to interrogate the Egyptian lunar record in the majority of chronological studies. Derstine (2016: 50; cf. Spalinger 2018: 10; Larsson and Larsson 2020) has argued for first evening crescent visibility (FCV) as the start of the lunar month *psḏntyw*. Notably, lunar day 1 appears to be the day of the FCV according to a Ramesses III lunar festival list.[15]

---

[14] I.e., first dawn of old crescent invisibility.

[15] Day 29 " ᶜḥᶜ... life time of the moon- end of the lunar month" if no crescent moon was seen; Day 30 "day of going forth of Min- whether or not it came to pass" the moon was seen on day 29 "; Day 1 " *psḏntyw* new day" the appearance of the first crescent; Day 2 "3bd Moon day" the day of the moon festival.

For year 24, *pśdntyw* can be interpreted as exactly on the mentioned date or one day later, viz. on II *prt* 30 or III *prt* 1 (Wente 1975: 267). If the last year of Thutmose IV was 1446 BC, then his accession would be ca. 1455 BC. Using the highest attested regnal years or "dead-reckoning" back to Amenhotep I (Gautchy 2014: 147), a chronology can be constructed (Table 2). Amenhotep I is subsequently 31 years earlier than the High Chronology and 56 years earlier than the Low Chronology.

With the accession date of 1535 BC for Thutmose III based solely on dead-reckoning (Table 2), the closest candidate to match the year 23 lunar record is accession 1529 BC. For the year 23 battle of Megiddo, exactly on I *šmw* 21, day 1 was 22nd May, 1507 BC. For year 24, III *prt* 1 was exactly *pśdntyw* on 2nd March, 1505 BC.

	Yrs.	Reign BC	
Amenhotep I	21	1581	1560
Thutmose I	13	1560	1547
Thutmose II	12	1547	1535
Hatshepsut	21	1535	1514
Thutmose III	54	1535	1481
Amenhotep II	26	1481	1455
Thutmose IV	9	1455	1446
Amenhotep III	38	1446	1408

Table 2: Chronology based on Thutmose IV terminus 1446 BC and dead-reckoning.

There are also lunar records for years 3, 20, and 21 of Amenhotep II. The year 3 record states that a ground breaking ceremony occurred on III *šmw* 15, presumably *pśdntyw*, while the year 20 record notes that grain was released for the brewing of beer on III *šmw* 6 for consumption, presumably on III *šmw* 9, 10 or 11 during the moon festival, and the year 21 record of II *šmw* 30 was a *psḏntyw* lunar day 1 festival (Gautschy 2014: 142; Derstine 2016: 45).

For years 3, 20 and 21 of Amenhotep II,[16] the closest match was year 3 III *šmw* 15, lunar day 1 on 7th July, 1476 BC, year 20 III *šmw* 12, which was *psḏntyw* on 30th June, 1459 BC, -1, and year 21 II *šmw* 30 was 18th June, 1458 BC, 1 day before *psḏntyw*, -1, with accession in 1478 BC. The reign of Amenhotep II is thought to be 26 or 37 years (Wente and Van Siclen III 1976: 248–50). If 1446 BC was the last year of Thutmose IV, then for a 26-year reign, a coregency would be required of about 3 years between Thutmose III and Amenhotep II, and a 4-year coregency between Amenhotep II and Thutmose IV.

An additional lunar record is Amenhotep III year 21 "feast of the valley" on lunar day 1 or day 2 on III *šmw* 1. Using the conventional calendar in the time frame of 1429-1422 BC, accession 1449-1442 BC (cf. Tompsett 2023: 4), there is a near match for accession 1442 BC where III *šmw* 1 started at dawn of the last visible crescent and III *šmw* 2 is *psḏntyw* on 11th June, 1422 BC. An alternative to Thutmose III accession 1529 BC is accession 1554 BC. For year 23, I *šmw* 21 was exactly *psḏntyw* on 28th May, 1532 BC. For year 24, III *prt* 1 was exactly *psḏntyw* on 9th March, 1530 BC.

The alternative interpretation of the record as II *prt* 30 would be on 8th March, 1530 BC, which was either last

---

[16] A year 3 date in 1473 BC would be lunar day 4 with the coregency of 3 years. The equivalent date is lunar day 1.

crescent or lunar disappearance, depending on latitude of observation or atmospheric extinction effects. Assuming accession for Amenhotep II was in 1500 BC, then year 3 was 1498 BC, year 20 was 1481 BC, and year 21 was 1480 BC. Year 3 III *šmw* 15 was lunar day 4, year 20 III *šmw* 9 was *pśdntyw* on 2nd July, one day early, -1, and year 21 II *šmw* 30 was lunar day 3 on 23rd June, 1480 BC.

If Amenhotep II had a three-year coregency with his father, year 3 III *šmw* 15 was 13th July, 1501 BC, and *pśdntyw*, year 20 III *šmw* 12 was *pśdntyw* on 6th July, -1, and year 21 II *šmw* 30 was 24th July, 1 day before lunar disappearance, -1. The reign of Amenhotep II requires an increase to 48 years, which is excessive, unless it is reduced to 37 years, and the reign of Thutmose IV is increased to 20 years.

However, if the last year of the reign of Thutmose IV was 1446 BC, the conventional reconstructed calendar results in a heliacal rising of Sirius that is too late in July, and therefore the Ebers and Khnum Sothic records suggest that the conventional reconstructed calendar is off between +14 to +18 days.[17] For Amenhotep I, the Ebers date of year 9 III *šmw* 9 - 14 days is II *šmw* 25, Elephantine Sothic date

---

[17] In this range of reductions all the solutions have lunar disappearance before the date of the heliacal rising of Sirius, 1 day before (-14 and -16) or 2 days before (-18), which is ca. 56 to ca. 76 years earlier than the traditional Sothic dates. A -12 calendar results in a short reign for Amenhotep II of less than 20 years, and is therefore unlikely.

was 12th July, 1574 BC, lunar day 2, supporting accession Amenhotep I in 1582 BC.

Thutmose III, year 23 I *šmw* 21 - 14 days was I *šmw* 7, which was exactly *psḏntyw* on 10th May, 1514 BC, accession 1536 BC. III šmw 28 - 14 was 12th July, 1498 BC with lunar disappearance on 10th July, or between 4 and 7 years later.

	Yrs.	**Reign BC**	
Amenhotep I	21	1582	1561
Thutmose I	12	1561	1549
Thutmose II	13	1549	1536
Hatshepsut	21	1536	1515
Thutmose III	54	1536	1482
Amenhotep II	30	1485	1455
Thutmose IV	9	1455	1446
Amenhotep III	38	1446	1408

Table 3: Chronology based on LD and -14 calendar.

	Yrs.	**Reign BC**	
Thutmose III	54	1536	1482
Amenhotep II	27	1485	1458
Thutmose IV	9	1458	1449
Coregent	3	1449	1446
Amenhotep III	38	1449	1411

Table 4: Alternate chronology for an unattested coregent based on LD and -14 calendar.

For the -14 LD calendar (Table 3), accession of Amenhotep II 1485 BC, year 3 III *šmw* 15 - 14 days is III *šmw* 1 and was *psḏntyw* (lunar day 1) on 25th June, 1482 BC, year 20 III *šmw* 11 - 14 days is II *šmw* 27, and *psḏntyw* on

17th June, 1466 BC, and year 21 II *šmw* 30 - 14 days was *psḏntyw* on 5th June, 1465 BC.

The lunar date of Amenhotep III (III šmw 1 - 14) day 1 or 2 falls on day 3 in 1426 BC, +1/+2, accession 1446 BC. However, there is an exact match for -14 LD for year 21 of Amenhotep III on 28th May, 1429 BC, accession 1449 BC (Table 4). Since Amenhotep III was only between the ages of 6 and 12 at his accession, a regent would have ruled until he was older,[18] and this unattested regent, according to this lunar solution and chronology, is a candidate for the Exodus Pharaoh.

	Yrs.	Reign BC	
Amenhotep I	21	1593	1572
Thutmose I	13	1572	1559
Thutmose II	12	1559	1547
Hatshepsut	21	1547	1526
Thutmose III	54	1547	1493
Amenhotep II	41	1496	1455
Thutmose IV	9	1455	1446
Amenhotep III	38	1446	1408

Table 5: Chronology based on LD and -16 calendar.

For the -16 LD calendar (Table 5), Amenhotep I accession 1593 BC, year 9 III *šmw* 9 - 16 days is II *šmw* 23, 12th July, 1585 BC, the Sothic date and the day of lunar disappearance, thus placing Thutmose III accession in 1547

---

[18] Bryan (2000: 253) remarks, "A regency by Mutemwiya appears unlikely, and, if the king was indeed a small child at accession, his rule was conducted for him quite unobtrusively. An alternative possibility might be that members of Queen Tiye's family assisted the king in his early rule."

BC. Year 23 I *šmw* 21 - 16 days is I *šmw* 5, which was exactly *psḏntyw* on 10th May, 1525 BC. For year 24, II *prt* 30 - 16 days is II *prt* 14, but *psḏntyw* was on II *prt* 16, 20th February, 1523 BC, -2, or -1 from III *prt* 1.

Khnum Elephantine III *šmw* 28 - 16 days would have to be a heliacal rising of Sirius on 12th July, 1509 BC, with lunar disappearance on either 11th or 12th July. However, observation of the heliacal rising of the star was feasible one day earlier, which would make the Sothic date 11th July between 1513 BC and 1510 BC without an associated lunar event. This does not impact the lunar date matches. Amenhotep II accession is 1496 BC, and year 3 III *šmw* 15 - 16 days is II *šmw* 29 on 26th June, 1494 BC, 1 day before *psḏntyw* (lunar disappearance), year 20 III *šmw* 11 - 16 days was 17th June, 1477 BC, 2 days before *psḏntyw*, and year 21 II *šmw* 30 - 16 days was 6th June, 1476 BC, 2 days before *psḏntyw*. The lunar fits for Amenhotep II are not particularly good, with -2, -1 and -2 for the three lunar records.

Assuming a 9-year reign for Thutmose IV results in an unusually long 41-year reign for Amenhotep II, though assigning 34 years to Amenhotep II and 18 to Thutmose IV with a 2-year coregency would explain a *Heb sed* renewal inscription for Amenhotep II and the year 19 wine docket for Thutmose IV, though this does not explain the *Heb sed* renewal inscriptions for Thutmose IV.

While the inscriptions may indeed have been just a preparation for the future, it might be conceivable that they planned to celebrate the anniversary of the finding of a stone in the shape of the 'divine falcon' as a young child. Thutmose IV relates this event in his inscription on the

Dream Stele found between the paws of the Great Sphinx at Giza (a monument he restored), on which he justified his rise to the Kingship (Clayton 1994: 113–114).

For the lunar record of Amenhotep III for -16 LD, there is a match on 26th May, 1426 BC, accession 1446 BC. Assuming that the *Heb sed* renewal inscriptions of Amenhotep II and Thutmose IV are not simply "unfulfilled wishes" but were actually celebrated in regnal year 34 may require the earliest possible Sothic solutions to account for the long reigns. A solution for the Sothic date of III *prt* 9 occurs in 1599 BC with a -16 calendar and LD observation method (Table 6), which places Amenhotep I accession in 1607 BC. The year 23 I *šmw* 21 lunar record of Thutmose III matches 1536 BC on 13th May, and year 24 II *prt* 30 1534 BC on 21st February.

	Yrs.	Reign BC	
Amenhotep I	21	1607	1587
Thutmose I	16	1587	1571
Thutmose II	13	1571	1558
Hatshepsut	21	1558	1537
Thutmose III	54	1558	1504
Amenhotep II	34	1507	1473
Thutmose IV	34	1480	1446
Amenhotep III	38	1446	1408
Akhenaten	17	1408	1391

Table 6: Chronology based on earliest Sothic solution and -16 calendar with LD.

These place his accession in 1558 BC. Amenhotep II year 3 III *šmw* 15 matches 1505 BC on 28th June, and year 20 III *šmw* 11 matches 1488 BC on 20th June, while year 21

II *šmw* 30 matches 1487 BC on 9th June. Subsequently, the accession of Amenhotep II is 1507 BC. Year 21 III *šmw* 1 of Amenhotep III matches 1426 BC on 26th May, accession 1446 BC. These results allow mentions of *Heb sed* renewals of 34 years in inscriptions for both Amenhotep II and Thutmose IV, but we have to entertain a coregency of 7 years. However, this construction in Table 6 is critically flawed because Thutmose IV appears to have died too young. It has been suggested from the evidence of the mummy of Thutmose IV that the pharaoh died at the age of about 35 (Wente 1995: 4).

The above model would require that Thutmose IV survived at least to the age of 35 years, which means that he would have been an infant when he considered himself to be the crown prince and very young when he gathered enough support to supplant his older brother when he succeeded Amenhotep II, etc. The lunar fits for the three lunar records of Amenhotep II are exact.

For the -14 FCV calendar (Table 7), Amenhotep I accession 1582 BC, an Elephantine Sothic date, year 9 III *šmw* 9 - 14 days is II *šmw* 25 on 12th July, 1574 BC, with first crescent on 13th July, -1, and lunar disappearance on 11th July, +1. For Thutmose III accession 1533 BC, year 23 III *šmw* 20 - 14 days is III *šmw* 6 on 8th May, 1511 BC, FCV on the evening before the battle on 23 I *šmw* 21 - 14 days, -1. For year 24, II *prt* 30 - 14 days is II *prt* 16 on 17th February, 1509 BC, FCV on evening of 24 II *prt* 29 - 14 days is II *prt* 15 on 16th February, 1509 BC, -1.

Khnum Elephantine III *šmw* 28 - 14 days is III *šmw* 14 on 12th July, 1498 BC, with lunar disappearance on III *šmw*

12, 10th July, and FCV on 12th July. The assumption is that a lunar date was of significance in the recording of the Sothic date, but at Elephantine, the heliacal rising of Sirius could have been observed on 11th July and, without an associated lunar date, could have been recorded 4 to 7 years later.

For accession Amenhotep II at 1482 BC, year 3 III *šmw* 15 - 14 days is III *šmw* 1 and was FCV on 23rd June, 1480 BC, year 20 III *šmw* 11 - 14 is II *šmw* 27 on 15th June, 1463 BC FCV, and year 21 II *šmw* 30 - 14 days was FCV on 5th June, 1462 BC.

	Yrs.	Reign BC	
Amenhotep I	21	1582	1561
Thutmose I	13	1561	1548
Thutmose II	15	1548	1533
Hatshepsut	21	1533	1512
Thutmose III	54	1533	1479
Amenhotep II	27	1482	1455
Thutmose IV	9	1455	1446
Amenhotep III	38	1446	1408

Table 7: Chronology based on FCV and -14 calendar.

An alternative chronology is Amenhotep II, 1482-1456 BC, and Thutmose IV, 1464-1446 BC. This coregency allows for the year 19 wine docket of Thutmose IV. For the year 21 lunar record for Amenhotep III, there is a match with FCV on 28th May, 1426 BC, accession 1446 BC. This would also be the last year of Thutmose IV, and this is also the result using -16 LD (above).

For the -16 FCV calendar (Table 8), accession of Amenhotep I is at 1590 BC, Ebers Sothic date III *šmw* 9 - 16 days is II *šmw* 23 on 12th July, 1582 BC, Sirius rising date and date of the first crescent moon 2 days after lunar disappearance 10th July. For Thutmose III accession 1544 BC, year 23 I *šmw* 21 - 16 days is I *šmw* 5 on 10th May, 1522 BC, which was FCV. For year 24, II *prt* 30 - 16 days was 17th February, 1520 BC and FCV.

Khnum Elephantine III *šmw* 28 - 16 days was III *šmw* 14 on 12th July, 1506 BC, and FCV+1, as 11th July was FCV. Or, Khnum Elephantine III *šmw* 28 - 16 days was III *šmw* 12 on 12th July, 1509 BC, FCV-1; FCV was 13th July. Or, Khnum Elephantine III *šmw* 28 - 16 days was III *šmw* 12 on 11th July, 1505 BC to 1502 BC with no matching new moon.

	Yrs.	Reign	BC
Amenhotep I	21	1590	1569
Thutmose I	13	1569	1556
Thutmose II	12	1556	1544
Hatshepsut	21	1544	1523
Thutmose III	54	1544	1490
Amenhotep II	38	1493	1455
Thutmose IV	12	1455	1443
Amenhotep III	38	1443	1405

Table 8: Chronology based on FCV and -16 calendar.

For the accession of Amenhotep II 1493 BC, year 3 III *šmw* 15 - 16 days is II *šmw* 29 and was FCV on 25th June, 1491 BC, year 20 III *šmw* 11 - 16 is II *šmw* 25, FCV on 17th June, 1474 BC and year 21 II *šmw* 30 - 16 days is II *šmw* 14, FCV on 5th June, 1473 BC. For the lunar record of Amenhotep III, there is a match with FCV on 10th June, 1423 BC, accession 1443 BC.[19]

---

[19] An Exodus date of 1443 BC requires 4th year of Solomon between 965-963 BC. Cf. Gedge (2022. Solomon 4th 964 BC,

Amenhotep II: Terminus 1446 BC

Although Amenhotep II as a candidate for Exodus Pharaoh has been shown above to have problems with the High Chronology, in view of the Egyptian and biblical historical records, it should be noted that Sothic and lunar fits are possible if his last year is placed at 1446 BC and the conventional reconstructed calendar is adjusted to -11 days using FCV[20] (Table 9).

	Yrs.	Reign	BC
Amenhotep I	21	1571	1550
Thutmose I	13	1550	1537
Thutmose II	12	1537	1525
Hatshepsut	21	1525	1504
Thutmose III	54	1525	1471
Amenhotep II	28	1475	1446
Thutmose IV	8	1446	1438
Amenhotep III	38	1438	1400

Table 9: Chronology based on FCV and -11 calendar.

Exodus 1444 BC); Gunneweg (1989. Jeroboam I 926-906 BC); Hayes and Hooker (2007. Jeroboam I 927-906 BC) and Hoeh (1983. Solomon 4th 965/64 BC, Exodus 1443 BC). An Exodus date of 1446 BC is based on 4th year Solomon 967 BC.

[20] A -9 LD calendar and observation method results in a solution but requires a reign of only 20 years, which is unlikely.

Figure 1. Fragments from KUB 19.15, Obv. II. Line 4'
mentions Ar-ma-a. Photo Phb10943 courtesy of Hethitologie-
Archiv Mainz.

Figure 2. *KUB 14.4/ IV 24* mentions a solar omen observed as Muršili II marched to Azzi. Photo BoFN00327 courtesy of Staatliche Museen Zu Berlin-Vorderasiatisches Museum.Bo 4802. *Rs.*

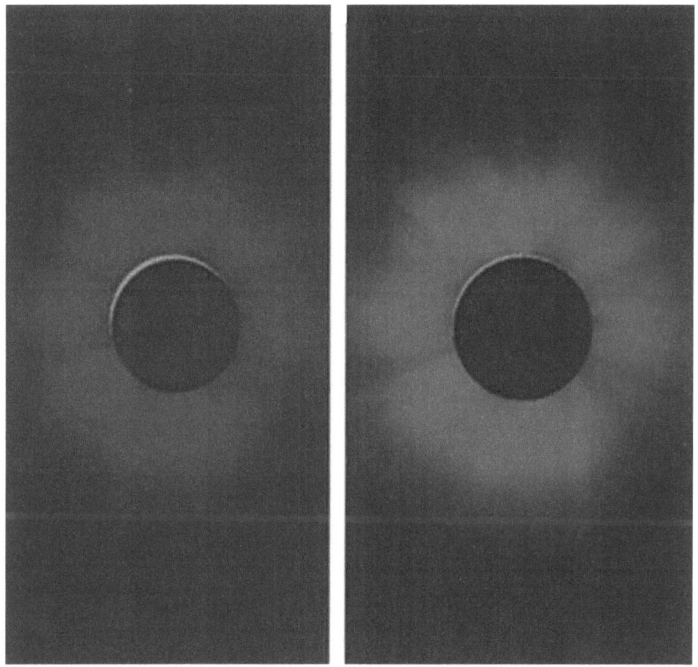

Figure 3. Left: Solar eclipse of 3rd May, 1375 BC at Ḫattuša (Boğazkale), magnitude 0.96, altitude 9° 31'. Right: The solar eclipse at Šamuḫa (Kayalıpınar), magnitude 0.98-0.99, altitude 10° 46'. Images courtesy of Starry Night Education.

Figure 4. Princess Neferurē‘ as a child, held by her tutor Senenmut. Photo courtesy of Trustees of the British Museum, EA 174.

Figure 5. Princess Neferurē' relief carved on the South
wall of the Bark Hall, Amun sanctuary of the memorial
temple of Hatshepsut at Deir el-Bahari. K. Kitchen
believed that the removal of the upper relief took place
between 1877-1894. Photo courtesy of Maciej Jawornicki.

Figure 6. Drawing of the relief of Princess Neferurē', South wall of the Bark Hall, Amun sanctuary of the memorial temple of Hatshepsut at Deir el-Bahari. Ippolito Rosellini, Monumenti storici, pl. XIX, 23, 1832.

Figure 7. Princess Neferurē' limestone relief that was removed from the South wall of the Bark Hall, Amun sanctuary of the memorial temple of Hatshepsut at Deir el-Bahari. Photo courtesy of Dundee's Art Gallery and Museum, 1977-534.

Figure 8. Princess Neferurē' dressed as an adult in white robe with scepter ḥts. Relief carved on the North wall of the Bark Hall, Amun sanctuary of the memorial temple of Hatshepsut at Deir el-Bahari. Photo courtesy of Maciej Jawornicki.

Figure 9. Drawing of stela of Princess Neferurēʻ, center, in long robe and wearing the double-feathered crown on a vulture headdress, followed by her tutor and steward Senenmut. Cairo JdE 38546; Sinai No. 179 from Serabit el-Khadim. A. H. Gardiner and T. E. Peet, The Inscriptions of Sinai I, pl. 68 no. 179, 1917.

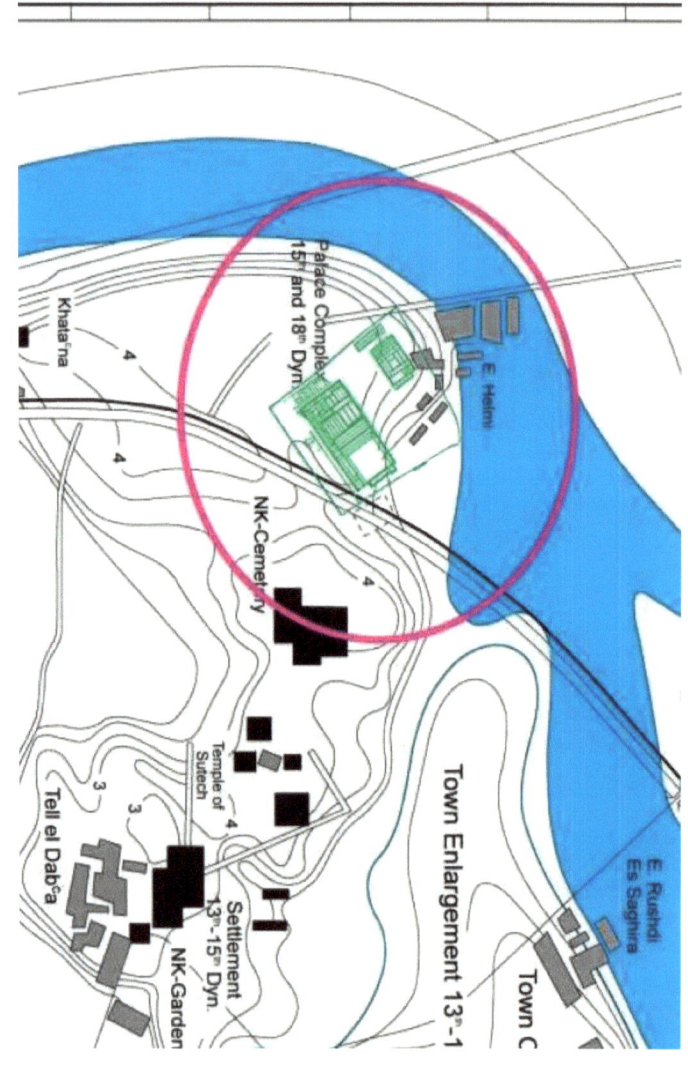

Figure 10. Avaris. Palace complex at 'Ezbet Helmy next to the Nile, circled. Drawing courtesy of Joint Archives of the Austrian Academy and the Austrian Archaeological Institute.

Figure 11. Reconstruction of the 18th Dynasty palatial complex at 'Ezbet Helmy. Drawing courtesy of Manfred Bietak, © Manfred Bietak.

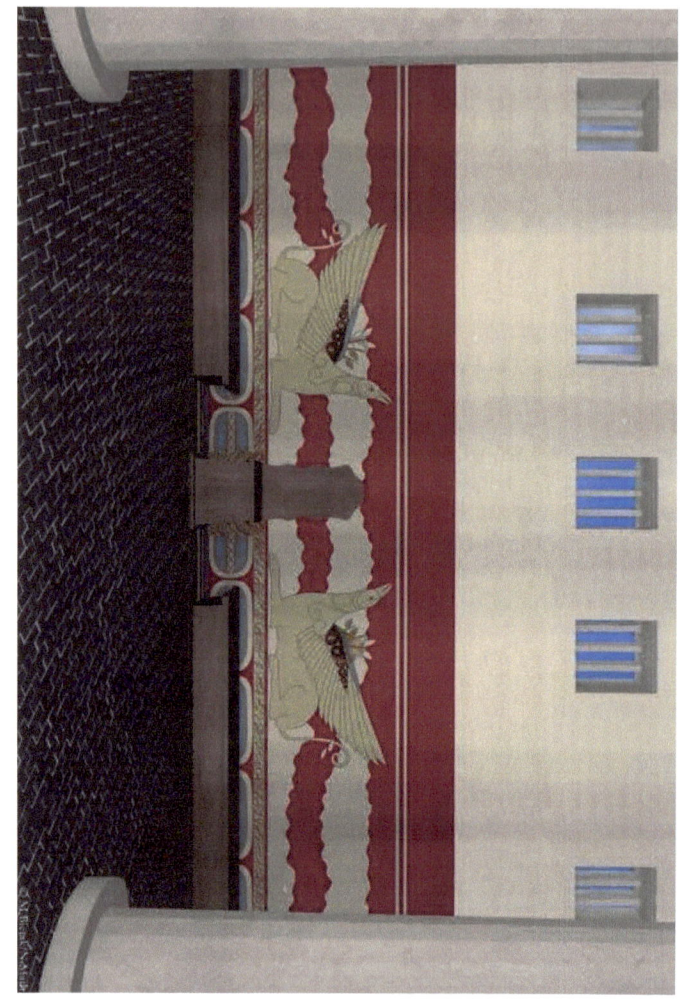

Figure 12. Reconstruction of the throne room of Palace F at 'Ezbet Helmy. Drawing courtesy of Manfred Bietak, © Manfred Bietak.

Figure 13. Thutmose IV in his chariot running down his Asiatic enemies, from Tomb KV43. National Museum of Egyptian Civilization in Cairo. Photo courtesy of B. O'Kane-Alamay.

Figure 14. Ceiling mural in Tomb KV 9 at the end of corridor G with two circles overlapping each other, which may represent a solar eclipse. Photo courtesy of Dr. Klaus Hentschel.

A heliacal rising of Sirius occurred on III *šmw* 9, 11th July, 1563 BC, accession Amenhotep I 1571 BC. For Thutmose III year 23, I *šmw* 21 - 11 days was I *šmw* 10 which was FCV on 10th May, 1503 BC, accession 1525 BC. For year 24, II *prt* 30 - 11 days was II *prt* 19, which was FCV on 18th February, 1501 BC. The Khnum Sothic date III *prt* 28 - 11 was apparently 12th July, 1487 BC, with the FCV on 11th July 1487 BC, the evening before.

For Amenhotep II, year 3 III *šmw* 15 - 11 days is III *šmw* 4 and was (lunar day 2) on 25th June, 1472 BC, accession 1475 BC,[21] year 20 III *šmw* 11 - 11 days is II *šmw* 30, and was FCV on 17th June, 1455 BC, and year 21 II *šmw* 30 - 11 days is II *šmw* 19 and was FCV on 5th June, 1454 BC.

For Amenhotep III, if accession was in 1438 BC, then year 21 lunar day 1 was either III *šmw* 1 or II *šmw* 30, - 11 days is II *šmw* 20 or 19 equivalent to 29th or 28th May, 1418 BC. FCV was on 29th May, 1418 BC. It has been seen in the above that moving the final year of Amenhotep II or Thutmose IV to 1446 BC impacts the reconstruction of the Egyptian calendar.

Amenhotep III to Ramesses II

The three conventional views for the accession of Ramesses II are: 1304 BC High Chronology, 1290 BC Middle Chronology, and 1279 BC Low Chronology. Huber

---

[21] Amenhotep II acceded to the throne on IV *3ḫt* day 1.
Accession 1475 BC is 2 years and 7 months earlier than the year 3 date in 1472 BC. 1474 BC is just over 1 year and 7 months.

(2011: 187) provided several candidates for year 1, which he concluded were fully supported by the recorded date: 1340 BC, 1315 BC, 1265 BC, and 1240 BC. Dead-reckoning from Thutmose IV ca. 1455-1446 BC results in Ramesses II, 1344 -1278 BC (Table 10; cf. Mahler 1890: 32–34).

	Yrs.	Reign BC	
Amenhotep III	38	1446	1408
Akhenaten	17	1408	1391
Smenkhkare	3	1391	1388
Neferneferuaten	2	1388	1386
Tutankhamun	10	1386	1376
Ay	4	1376	1372
Horemheb	15	1372	1357
Ramesses I	2	1357	1355
Seti I	11	1355	1344
Ramesses II	66	1344	1278

Table 10: Dead-reckoning Amenhotep III to Ramesses II.

	Yrs.	Reign BC	
Amenhotep III	38	1446	1408
Akhenaten	17	1408	1391
Smenkhkare	3	1391	1388
Neferneferuaten	2	1388	1386
Tutankhamun	10	1386	1376
Ay	8	1376	1368
Horemheb	15	1368	1353
Ramesses I	2	1353	1351
Seti I	11	1351	1340
Ramesses II	66	1340	1274

Table 11: Ramesses II 1340 BC; conventional calendar.

Accession dates from year 52 solutions that are marginally supported are: 1329 BC, 1304 BC, 1290 BC,

1279 BC, and 1254 BC (Huber 2011: 187). For the conventional calendar (Table 11), one solution for the primary lunar record of year 52 for Ramesses II is II *prt* 27, which was exactly *pśdntyw* on 3rd January, 1288 BC, accession 1340 BC.[22]

There is also a secondary lunar record for year 47 of Ramesses II, which is II *prt* 25 for lunar day 4 or 5.

	Yrs.	**Reign BC**	
Amenhotep III	38	1446	1408
Akhenaten	17	1408	1391
Smenkhkare	3	1391	1388
Neferneferuaten	2	1388	1386
Tutankhamun	10	1386	1376
Ay	4	1376	1372
Horemheb	14	1372	1358
Ramesses I	1	1358	1357
Seti I	10	1357	1347
Ramesses II	66	1347	1281

Table 12: Ramesses II 1347 BC; LD and -14 calendar.

This matches II *prt* 25 and day 5, and II *prt* 21 was *pśdntyw* on 30th December, 1294 BC. For the -14 LD calendar (Table 12), Ramesses II accession is 1347 BC, year 52 II *prt* 27 - 14 days was II *prt* 13, which was exactly *pśdntyw* on 22nd December, 1296 BC. For year 47, II *prt* 25 - 14 days was II *prt* 11 on 21st December, 1301 BC, with lunar disappearance on 16th December, 1301 BC. II *prt* 11 was day 6, +1.

---

[22] Also, II *prt* 27 8th January, 1302 BC, accession 1353 BC.

For the -16 LD calendar (Table 13), Ramesses II accession 1333 BC, year 52 II *prt* 27 - 16 days was II *prt* 11, which was exactly *pśdntyw* on 17th December, 1282 BC.

	Yrs.	Reign BC	
Amenhotep III	39	1446	1407
Akhenaten	17	1407	1390
Smenkhkare	3	1390	1387
Neferneferuaten	2	1387	1385
Tutankhamun	9	1385	1376
Ay	4	1376	1372
Horemheb	27	1372	1345
Ramesses I	1	1345	1344
Seti I	11	1344	1333
Ramesses II	66	1333	1267

Table 13: Ramesses II 1333 BC; LD and -16 calendar.

For year 47, II *prt* 25 - 16 days was II *prt* 9, and II *prt* 6 was lunar disappearance on 13th December, 1287 BC. Year 47 II *prt* 9 was therefore day 4. For the -14 FCV calendar (Table 14), Ramesses II accession is 1344 BC, year 52 II *prt* 27 - 14 days was II *prt* 13 on 21st December, 1293 BC, and year 52 II *prt* 26 or 27 - 14 days was FCV on evening of 20th or 21st December, 1293 BC. For year 47, II *prt* 25-14 that is II, *prt* 11 and was 21st December in 1298 BC. Since FCV was on II *prt* 6 on 16th December in year 47. Then II *prt* 11 was day 6, a day later than expected.

For the -16 FCV calendar (Table 15), there are no exact matches for year 52 of Ramesses II in the acceptable time frame with an accession between 1348-1334 BC.

	Yrs.	Reign BC	
Amenhotep III	38	1446	1408
Akhenaten	17	1408	1391
Smenkhkare	3	1391	1388
Neferneferuaten	2	1388	1386
Tutankhamun	10	1386	1376
Ay	4	1376	1372
Horemheb	15	1372	1357
Ramesses I	2	1357	1355
Seti I	11	1355	1344
Ramesses II	66	1344	1278

Table 14 : Ramesses II 1344 BC; FCV and -14 calendar.

	Yrs.	Reign BC	
Amenhotep III	38	1443	1405
Akhenaten	17	1408	1391
Smenkhkare	3	1391	1388
Neferneferuaten	2	1388	1386
Tutankhamun	10	1386	1376
Ay	4	1376	1372
Horemheb	15	1372	1357
Ramesses I	2	1357	1355
Seti I	11	1355	1344
Ramesses II	66	1344	1278

Table 15: Ramesses II accession 1344 BC (-1); FCV and -16 calendar.

This may reflect an observational error or perhaps a calendar reform sometime after Amenhotep III. The best alternative is a -1 miss, viz. accession 1344 BC, where year 52 II *prt* 27 - 16 days was II *prt* 11 on 19th December, 1293 BC, and 20th December first crescent, -1.

For year 47, II *prt* 25 was 19th December, 1298 BC - 16 days was II *prt* 9 and FCV was II *prt* 6 on 16th December, 1298 BC. II *prt* 6 was therefore day 4 exactly.

	Yrs.	Reign BC	
Amenhotep III	38	1438	1400
Akhenaten	17	1400	1383
Smenkhkare	3	1383	1380
Neferneferuaten	2	1380	1378
Tutankhamun	9	1378	1369
Ay	4	1369	1364
Horemheb	27	1364	1337
Ramses I	1	1337	1336
Seti I	11	1336	1325
Ramesses II	66	1325	1259

Table 16: Ramesses II accession 1325 BC; FCV and -11 calendar.

	Yrs.	Reign BC	
Amenhotep III	38	1438	1400
Akhenaten	17	1408	1391
Smenkhkare	3	1391	1388
Neferneferuaten	2	1388	1386
Tutankhamun	10	1386	1376
Ay	4	1376	1372
Horemheb	26	1372	1346
Ramses I	1	1346	1345
Seti I	9	1345	1336
Ramesses II	66	1336	1270

Table 17: Ramesses II accession 1336 BC; FCV and -11 calendar.

For Amenhotep II terminus 1446 BC based on a -11 calendar with FCV, there are two possible solutions. II *prt* 27 - 11 days matches the FCV on 20th December, 1274 BC, accession Ramesses II 1325 BC (Table 16). Also, II *prt* 27 - 11 days is FCV on 22nd December, 1285 BC, accession Ramesses II 1336 BC (Table 17).

Akhetaten Boundary Stelae

In addition to the Sothic and lunar records, boundary stelae from the city of Akhet-Aten (modern Amarna) record that the king (Akhenaten) took an oath to found the city. The date on three earlier stelae reads year 5 IV *prt* 13 and year 6 IV *prt* 13. This is possible for a solar date but not for a lunar date. According to Hornung (2001: 62), "the date chosen was that on which, for an observer, the rising sun shone directly into the length of the… mortuary temple of the king, from an indentation in the eastern horizon."

The original observation by Akhenaten on IV *prt* 13 in year 5 and again in year 6 was likely to be on 5th March, but would by year 12 on completion of the observation platform, occur on the 3rd of March, and by year 17 have slipped to 2nd March. According to the traditional Egyptian calendar, this would place the accession of Akhenaten between 1353 BC and 1351 BC. In contrast, Garcia (2019: 75) argued that an "alignment might have taken place on 2nd March in the year 1335 BC with an error margin of 4 years."

The basic assumptions are that the Egyptian calendar of 365 days remained unaltered throughout the Egyptian Dynastic period, the event took place on IV *prt* 13 between 5th March 1349 and 2nd March 1335 BC, and not again on those dates until a further 1460 Egyptian years had elapsed. However, if the calendar was changed for any reason, this would no longer hold true. With a -11, -14 or -16 day calendar shift as proposed above, the event would have occurred 44, 56 or 64 years earlier, respectively. Within the constraints of the model chronologies proposed above, they would be incompatible with the initial Horizon of the Aten in year 5, occurring on 2nd March.

Table 18 summarizes the possible solar alignments at Akhet-Aten with different Egyptian calendars. Calendar 0 is the conventional reconstructed calendar using the Low Chronology.

Calendar	Yr 5 BC		Accession BC	
0	1349	1347	1353	1351
-11	1393	1391	1397	1395
-14	1405	1403	1409	1407
-16	1413	1411	1417	1415

Table 18: The range of solar alignments for year 5, IV *prt* 13-X on 5th March at the city of Akhet-Aten with subsequent ranges of accession dates for Akhenaten using various Egyptian calendar modifications from 0 to -16 days. Had the solar event taken place on 2nd March these calendar dates would be 12 years later.

The conventional calendar with Low Chronology for Akhenaten 1353-1336 BC has a solution on 5th March, accession between 1353 BC and 1351 BC. The High Chronology with Akhenaten 1370-1353 BC has no fit on 5th March, unless the observation is moved to 9th March, which is unlikely. The -14 calendars with Akhenaten 1408-1391 BC (Tables 12 and 14; Thutmose IV 1455-1446 BC), have a solution for 5th March, with accession Akhenaten between

1409 BC and 1407 BC. The -16 calendars with Akhenaten accession 1408 BC or 1405 BC (Tables 5 and 8; Thutmose IV alternative) do not have a fit on 5th March, unless the observation is moved to 3rd March, or there is a coregency of ca. 9 years. The -11 calendars with accession Akhenaten 1408 BC or 1400 BC (Tables 16 and 17; Amenhotep II 1475-1446 BC), have no fit for 5th March, unless the reign of Amenhotep III is increased 3-5 years, which is unlikely, or the observation is moved to either 6th March (Table 16) or 8th March (Table 17). But as noted above, the original observation was likely on 5th March. For the theory of an unattested coregent (Table 4), one would have to posit a reign of 40 years for Amenhotep III.

Tell el-Amarna Letters

An additional synchronism of interest may be found in the Tell el-Amarna Letters, which are 382 tablets spanning 15 to 30 years, dated mostly to the reigns of Amenhotep III and Akhenaten, with some dating to Tutankhamun. The letters are often filled with requests by Canaanite city-kings ("mayors") to the Pharaoh asking for help against an invading people in Canaan known as the ʿApîru/Ḫabiru. The Amarna Letters often describe the ʿApîru/Ḫabiru as conquering the Canaanite territories *en masse* (Eames 2023: 29), without significant Egyptian interference (e.g., EA 137). In EA 286, ʿAbdi-Ḫeba, mayor of Jerusalem, writes, "Lost are all the mayors; there is not a mayor remaining…The Ḫabiru has plundered all the lands of the king."

The contents of the letters have suggested to many that some (1/5) of the ʿApîru/Ḫabiru are the Israelite-Hebrews (e.g., Wood 1997: 245–256; Stripling 2021: 38–39; Eames 2023: 28–33; Billington 2024: 14–16). Ramesses II (Berlin Pedestal) ca. 1250 BC or 1315 BC (-14 FCV), and Merneptah (Israel Stele) ca. 1210 BC or 1275 BC (-14 FCV), had an enemy people in Canaan they knew as "Israel."

A biblical year for the Israelite Conquest of Canaan is 1406 BC, and the end of Joshua's military activity occurred sometime in 1400 BC[23] (Steinmann 2011: 89). The -14 and -16 LD chronologies place the accession of Akhenaten at ca. 1408 BC.[24] In Josh 10:1, the ruler of Jerusalem at the beginning of the conquest was Adoni-Zedek, so 'Abdi-Ḥeba appears to be a later replacement. The Amarna Letters indicate that Pharaoh appointed replacement mayors for those killed by the 'Apîru/Ḥabiru and also by their Canaanite/ Amorite allies (Billington 2024: 15).

Tablet EA 254 (VAT 335) was written by the mayor of Shechem, named Lab'ayu, in which he defends the charge that his son was consorting with the Ḥabiru. In EA 289 'Abdi-Ḥeba, the mayor of Uru-Salim [Jerusalem],

---

[23] However, as Windle (2025b) noted, "[T]he attempts by various tribes to conquer their allotted territories lasted into the period of the Judges."

[24] If terminus of either Amenhotep II or Thutmose IV was 1446 BC, then accession Akhenaten was 1400 BC or 1408 BC, respectively. The second half of the reign of Amenhotep III and Akhenaten are often labeled LB IIA, but if the LB IB destructions in Canaan are from the Israelites beginning in 1406 BC, and the 'Apîru/Ḥabiru Conquest of Canaan is the Israelites, then late Amenhotep III and or early Akhenaten should perhaps be dated LB IB, rather than LB IIA.

complains that Lab'ayu gave the land of Šakmu [Shechem] to the Ḫabiru. In Josh 24:1, the Israelites appear to be at peace with Shechem. EA 254 can be dated, since it has a hieratic docket written in ink by an Egyptian scribe at the base of the tablet, but which is very poorly preserved (cf. Mynářová 2011: 124; Dodson 2014: 81). Knudtzon (1915: 812; Helck 1962: 188; Na'aman 1975: 214; Cochavi-Rainey 2005: 194; Kennedy 2011: 44) read "year 10 (+) 2," and Rainey (2015: 1033) "year 10 + 2 (+ X?)," while Albright (1947: 59; 1966: 5) reads "year 30 (+) 2." The reading of "year 10 (+) 2" would be year 12 of Akhenaten, while "year 30 (+) 2" would be year 32 of Amenhotep III (cf. Moran 1992: xxxvii).

The Low Chronology for Amenhotep III is 1391-1353 BC, and year 32 is 1360 BC, while the Low Chronology for Akhenaten is 1353-1336 BC, with year 12 being 1342 BC. These Low Chronology dates for EA 254 are thus 46-64 years after the beginning of the 1406 BC conquest. The High Chronology for Amenhotep III is 1407-1370 BC, and year 32 would be 1376 BC, while the High Chronology for Akhenaten is 1370-1353 BC, with year 12 being 1359 BC.

With Thutmose IV ca. 1455-1446 BC, year 12 of Akhenaten would be ca. 1397 BC, while year 32 of Amenhotep III would be ca. 1415 BC, which is prior to the Israelite conquest, unless there was a 9-year coregency with Akhenaten.[25] For Amenhotep II 1475-1446 BC, year 12 of

---

[25] Martín-Valentín and Bedman (2017: 377); cf. Johnson (1996: 80–82); contra Brand (2020: 59), suggest an 8 or 9-year coregency of Akhenaten and Amenhotep III. Year 12 would then be 1406 BC or 1405 BC. An example chronology: Amenhotep

Akhenaten would be 1389 BC, while year 32 of Amenhotep III would be 1407 BC. Since the month and day for the accession of Amenhotep III is unknown, a precise range for year 32 is not possible. His first, second, and third jubilee dates are II *šmw* 27 (year 30), I *šmw* 1 (year 34), and IV *3ḫt* 30 (year 37). If we assume that II *šmw* 27 was on the anniversary of his accession date, year 32 would run from late May 1407 BC to late May 1406 BC.

The Israelites crossed the Jordan River 10th Abib/Nisan, 1406 BC (Josh 4:19), and Jericho fell no earlier than 28th Abib/Nisan (Josh 6:15; Steinmann 2011: 88–89), so with these assumptions, year 32 would just barely overlap the first month of the conquest. However, it is unlikely that EA 254 is describing events in the first month of the conquest of Canaan, since Lab'ayu is replying to pharaoh concerning a complaint against him that his son had been "consorting with the 'Apîru." Thus, for the complaint to have reached Pharaoh, for Pharaoh's response to Lab'ayu, and then for Lab'ayu's response to Pharaoh in EA 254 would have taken a period of at least 6 months to possibly a couple of years.

Therefore, the reading "year 10 (+) 2" is superior to "year 30 (+) 2" for both Thutmose IV and Amenhotep II with terminus 1446 BC.

III 1446-1408 BC Akhenaten 1417-1400 BC Neferneferuaten 1400-1393 BC Smenkhkare 1393-1386 BC Tutankhamun 1386-1376 BC Ay 1376-1372 BC. For Akhenaten 1417-1400 BC, solar alignment on IV *prt* 13 would be 5th March for -16 chronologies, but 7th March (too late) for -14 chronologies.

Solar Omen of Muršili II

The information in the fragmentary Hittite text KUB 19.15 + KBo 50.24 (Figure 1), presented at a conference in 2005 (Miller 2008: 533–554), and dated to years 7 to 9 of Muršili II has been interpreted as containing a synchronism with either year 1 of Pharaoh Ay or year 1 of Pharaoh Horemheb, the former being the more likely (Devecci and Miller 2011: 157; Gautschy 2014: 148). The relevant portion of the tablet (Miller 2007: 253) reads:

[But when] Ḫ[...] sat [upon the throne of] ki[ngship]
'Arma'a began t[hereup]on to take [ve]ngeance upon
A[murru].

It is believed that 'Arma'a is Horemheb,[26] with the one ascending to the throne being Ay. While only Ḫ[...] is preserved, Ay's throne name, Ḫeper-ḫepru-re,[27] is a favored candidate. Another Hittite record from the Annals of Muršili II for year 9/10 (Figure 2) has been interpreted that a solar omen was observed at the time he was marching to Azzi-Ḫayaša with his army (Huber 2001: 644), and the old queen tried to use the omen to depose him.

[When] I was marching [toward the land A]zzi – Now the
Sun-god made an omen.

---

[26] Ar-ma-a may be a representation of Ḫarmaḫa. In the later Manethonian tradition, Horemheb is called Armais, Armesis, Armaios and Harmais.

[27] Miller (2011: 156) suggests Ḫur-riya as a possible shortened form.

The solar omen has been interpreted as a solar eclipse. The exact location during the military march is unknown, although it was apparently observed between Ḫattuša and the land of Azzi-Ḫayaša, a land "thought to be situated in the north-east of Anatolia, somewhere around the Lake Van" (Gautschy 2014: 149). It is not known what time of year it may have occurred, though spring appears to be a likely season to begin a military campaign. The reign for Ay in the conventional High Chronology is 1338-1334 BC, and 1323-1319 BC for the Low Chronology, and the reign for Horemheb is 1334-1307 BC for the High Chronology, and 1319-1292 BC for the Low Chronology.

Candidates for the solar eclipse for the conventional chronology according to Gautschy (2011: 148) are 13th April, 1308 BC, 24th June, 1312 BC, 17th October, 1328 BC, 13th March, 1335 BC, 8th January, 1340 BC, and 16th October, 1355 BC. She concludes that "1312 BC, 1328 BC and 1355 BC are not compatible with the interpretation of the text that Muršili started campaigning around the time of the eclipse" (2014: 148).

For the solar eclipse of 8th January, 1340 BC, it is unlikely that Muršili II would have been on a campaign in January. Candidate 13th March, 1335 BC had a magnitude of 0.89-0.92 at 39° altitude and aligns with the beginning of the reign of Horemheb using the High Chronology.

		Ḫattuša	Alt	Šamuḫa
-1391	11-Apr	0.19	27	0.17
-1390	24-Sep	0.93	13	0.91
-1389	20-Feb	0.48	23	0.47
-1388	9-Feb	0.70	17	0.73
-1386	8-Dec	0.26	3	0.15
-1383	12-May	0.61	28	0.64
-1381	15-Sep	0.91	54	0.94
-1377	5-Jul	0.69	15	0.72
-1374	3-May	0.96	10	0.98
-1368	24-Jul	0.40	8	0.40
-1365	23-May	0.52	22	0.52
-1362	15-Sep	0.45	<1	0.47
-1361	12-Mar	0.78	30	0.76
-1359	15-Jul	0.86	44	0.83
-1355	27-Oct	0.49	19	0.50
-1354	16-Oct	0.30	19	0.30
-1351	15-Aug	0.40	53	0.39
-1350	30-Dec	0.29	13	0.30
-1344	2-Apr	0.26	49	0.30
-1339	8-Jan	1.00	25	1.00
-1337	14-May	0.66	48	0.67
-1334	13-Mar	0.89	39	0.92
-1331	30-Dec	0.41	17	0.39
-1327	17-Oct	0.75	37	0.73
-1314	26-Aug	0.70	26	0.71
-1311	24-Jun	0.99	64	0.98
-1308	17-Oct	0.48	13	0.48
-1307	13-Apr	0.22	<7	0.30
-1305	17-Aug	0.50	67	0.52
-1295	31-Jan	0.46	29	0.34
-1289	24-Apr	0.31	49	0.17

Table 19: Solar eclipses with magnitude and altitude at Ḫattuša and with magnitude at Šamuḫa.

For the solar eclipse of 17th October, 1328 BC, 0.75 magnitude is at the lowest detection limit.[28] The suggestion of Miller (Devecci and Miller 2011: 167) of 26th August, 1315 BC, magnitude 0.70 at 26° altitude, is also slightly below the detection limit, and this candidate occurs in the reign of Horemheb.

For spring solar eclipses, not listed by Gautschy is 14th May, 1338 BC, which is a candidate for Ay with the High Chronology, but at magnitude 0.66 and an altitude of 48° it would likely not have been observed. Candidate 13th April, 1308 BC aligns with the reign of Horemheb in the high or low chronologies, but was a sunrise solar eclipse of only 0.22 magnitude where 12% was eclipsed when it rose above the mountains at Ḫattuša (Gautschy 2017a: 26). This would therefore likely have missed detection.

A spring solar eclipse candidate for the low or high chronologies that would likely have been observed is arguably absent. Dead-reckoning from Thutmose IV ca. 1455-1446 BC forward 70 years (cf. Gautschy 2014: 147) places Ay at ca. 1376-1372 BC. If this placement of Thutmose IV is correct, a spring solar eclipse around this time that would have been observed ca. 1375 BC is expected, and the candidate is there. The solar eclipse of 3rd May, 1375 BC was 0.96 magnitude and 9° altitude at Ḫattuša, and 0.98-

---

[28] Ginzel (1899) held a lower limit of 0.8 magnitude at high altitude and a lower limit of 0.6 magnitude near the horizon. More recent suggestions by Muller and Stephenson (1975: 463–467) are a lower limit of 0.95 magnitude at high altitude. See also Roaf (2012: 163).

0.99 magnitude at Šamuḫa[29] (Figure 3), a town on the way to Azzi. This is the only spring solar eclipse between 1392-1290 BC that likely would have been observed (Table 19).

For the alternative solution of Amenhotep II 1475-1446 BC and Ramesses II accession 1325 BC (Table 16), Ay would reign ca. 1369-1364 BC. Two possible candidates are the summer solar eclipse of 24th July, 1369 BC at 0.40 magnitude and 8° altitude, and the spring eclipse of 23rd May, 1366 BC, 0.52 magnitude and 22° altitude, though both of these solar eclipses are below the theoretical detection limit. The alternative would be to suggest a coregency between Amenhotep III and Akhenaten of 8 years (Table 17), which would place Ay at 1376-1372 BC, and the solar eclipse candidate would then be 3rd May, 1375 BC, magnitude 0.96-0.99. The possibility of a coregency between these two pharaohs has been much debated, with the consensus unconvinced of a coregency (Berman 1998: 23).

Daḫamunzu Affair

Before the recently discovered synchronism between Muršili II and Ay or Horemheb, the Daḫamunzu-affair was the principal synchronism between Egypt and the Hittites before Ramesses II. In the *Deeds of Šuppiluliuma* (DŠ), Muršili II says that he received a letter from the Egyptian queen, called by her title daḫamunzu, that her husband had

---

[29] P. J. Huber's Solec program gives 0.995 magnitude at Šamuḫa. A decrease in ΔT of 23 minutes will produce totality at Ḫattuša.

died and that they had no son. This occurred while his father. Šuppiluliuma I was in the land of Karkemiš. She asked Šuppiluliuma to send one of his sons. The Pharaoh who had just died is thought to be either Akhenaten, Tutankhamun, or Smenkhkare.

Though each candidate has found supporters, the predominate opinion is that the Pharaoh in question was Tutankhamun. The likely reign lengths of the Hittite kings are: Šuppiluliuma I 25-35 years, Arnuwanda 2 years, Muršili II 25-31 years, Muwatalli 18-23 years, Muršili III 7 years, and Hattušili III 25-30 years.

Year	Egypt	Ḫatti
1446	Amenhotep III	
1410		Šuppiluliuma I
1408	Akhenaten	
1391	Smenkhkare	
1388	Neferneferuaten	
1386	Tutankhamun	
1385		Arnuwanda
1384		Muršili II
1376	Ay	
1372	Horemheb	
1358		Muwatalli
1357	Ramesses I	
1355	Seti I	
1344	Ramesses II	
1340		Muršili III
1333		Hattušili III

Table 20: Chronology and synchronisms between Egypt and Ḫatti based on year 9/10 Muršili II solar omen with the solar eclipse of 3rd May, 1375 BC and year 8/9 with year 1 Ay.

The synchronisms with Egypt require that Muwatalli was alive in year 5 of Ramesses II, Hattušili III as king before year 21 of Ramesses II, and Hattušili III was still alive after year 34 of Ramesses II (Gautschy 2014: 148).

In the above chronology (Table 20) based on dead-reckoning from the solar eclipse of 3rd May, 1375 BC, the reign of Šuppiluliuma is 1410-1385 BC, and Akhenaten died in 1391 BC. However, if the Pharaoh was Tutankhamun, there would be no synchronism with Šuppiluliuma. The candidates are therefore reduced to Smenkhkare or Akhenaten. Akhenaten and his wife Nefertiti had daughters but no male heir, while Smenkhkare and his wife Meritaten had no children. Nefertiti is not mentioned in the Amarna letters, while Meritaten is mentioned twice in letters from the Babylonian king. With the two-year reign of Lady Neferneferuaten following Smenkhkare, the situation may suggest that Meritaten is the queen mentioned in the DŠ (Willhem and Boese 1987: 74–117; Gautschy 2014: 151).

The lack of a reliable Sothic record for Ramesses II makes it difficult to determine the exact calendar being used at the time. With the absolute date for the accession of Ay at 1376 BC, dead-reckoning provides accession of Ramesses II between ca. 1348-1334 BC. The accessions of Ramesses II that have exact matches of the lunar records are: 1333 BC (-16 LD), 1340 BC (conventional, LD), 1344 BC (-14 FCV), and 1347 BC (-14 LD). While an in-depth study of the synchronisms between Egypt, Assyria, and Babylonia are beyond the scope of this study, it may nevertheless be helpful to provide absolute chronologies documented in Egyptian, Assyrian, and Babylonian sources (Table 21).

Year	Egypt	Assyria	Babylonia
1481	Amenhotep II		
1476		Enlil-nāṣir II	
1470		Aššur-nīrārī II	Kara-indaš
1463		Aššur-bēl-nišēšu	
1461			Kadašman Harbe I
1455	Thutmose IV		
1453		Aššur-rā'im-nišešu	
1452			Kurigalzu I
1446	Amenhotep III	Aššur-nādin-aḫḫe II	
1436		Erība Adad I	
1423			Kadašman-Enlil I
1409		Aššur-uballiṭ I	Burnaburiaš
1408	Akhenaten		
1407			
1382			Kara-hardaš
1382			Nazi-Bugaš
1376	Ay		
1372	Horemheb	Enlil-nīrārī	
1362		Arik-dēn-ili	
1359			
1358	Ramses I		
1356			Nazi-Maruttaš
1355	Seti I	Adad-nīrarī I	
1344	Ramesses II		
1336			
1330			Kadašman Turgu I
1329			
1319		Šalmaneser I	

Table 21: Absolute chronologies for Egypt, Assyria and Babylonia based on year 9/10 Muršili II solar omen with the solar eclipse of 3rd May, 1375 BC, where year 8/9 Muršili II is year 1 Ay.

Ramesses II to Shoshenq I

What has not been addressed in previous editions is the chronological gap created by moving the 18th Dynasty earlier. For Ramesses II the difference between 1344 BC (dead-reckoning, and -14 FCV) or 1333 BC (-16 LD) and the Low Chronology date of 1279 BC is ca. 54-65 years. With the anchor date for Shoshenq I of ca. 943-922 BC,[30] additional regnal years totaling 54 to 65 years are thus required between these two pharaohs. While an in-depth review of the relevant data is beyond the scope of this study, some initial suggestions for further research can be put forward.

For the first king of the 21st Dynasty, Smendes, the inscriptions provide the highest date of year 25, while Manetho gives 26 years. For Amenemnisu, Manetho provides 4 years. Manetho, according to Eusebius, gives a reign of 41 years to Psusennes I, while Africanus provides 46 years, though inscriptional evidence suggests 48+ years (e.g., Wente 1967: 168, 171–173). For his successor, Amenemope, Manetho gives a reign of 9 years. However, a mummy-bandage has the inscription: "King of Upper and Lower Egypt Amenemope, linen made by the High Priest of Amun X for his lord Amun in Year 49" (Niwiński 1979: 56–57).

---

[30] Based on the invasion of Shoshenq I in his 20th year of Israel and Judah in Rehoboam's 5th year, 926 BC.

	Pharaoh	Yrs. BC		Reign
	Ay	1376	1372	4
	Horemheb	1372	1357	15
19th	Ramesses I	1357	1355	2
	Seti I	1355	1344	11
	Ramesses II	1344	1278	66
	Merneptah	1278	1268	10
	Amenmesse	1268	1264	4
	Seti II	1264	1258	6
	Siptah	1258	1252	6
	Twosre	1252	1250	2
20th	Sethnakht	1250	1247	3
	Ramesses III	1247	1216	31
	Ramesses IV	1216	1209	7
	Ramesses V	1209	1204	5
	Ramesses VI	1204	1196	8
	Ramesses VII	1196	1188	8
	Ramesses VIII	1188	1187	1
	Ramesses IX	1187	1169	18
	Ramesses X	1169	1165	4
	Ramesses XI	1165	1135	30
21st	Smendes	1135	1109	26
	Psusennes I	1109	1060	49
	Amenemnisut	1060	1056	4
	Amenemope	1056	1004	52
	Osorkon	1004	988	16
	Siamun	988	969	19
	Psusennes II	969	945	24
22nd	Shoshenq I	945	924	21

Table 22: Dead-reckoning from Ay (solar eclipse 3rd May, 1375 BC).

	Pharaoh	Yrs. BC		Reign
	Ay	1376	1372	4
	Horemheb	1372	1345	27
19th	Ramesses I	1345	1344	2
	Seti I	1344	1333	11
	Ramesses II	1333	1267	66
	Merneptah	1267	1257	10
	Amenmesse	1257	1253	4
	Seti II	1253	1247	6
	Siptah	1247	1241	6
	Twosre	1241	1239	2
20th	Sethnakht	1239	1236	3
	Ramesses III	1236	1205	31
	Ramesses IV	1205	1198	7
	Ramesses V	1198	1193	5
	Ramesses VI	1193	1185	8
	Ramesses VII	1185	1177	8
	Ramesses VIII	1177	1176	1
	Ramesses IX	1176	1158	18
	Ramesses X	1158	1154	4
	Ramesses XI	1154	1124	30
21st	Smendes	1124	1098	26
	Psusennes I	1098	1049	49
	Amenemnisut	1049	1045	4
	Amenemope	1045	993	52
	Osorkon	993	987	6
	Siamun	987	968	19
	Psusennes II	968	944	24
22nd	Shoshenq I	944	923	21

Table 23: Dead-reckoning from Ay (solar eclipse 3rd May, 1375 BC), or Ramesses II 1333 BC (-16 LD calendar).

In addition, an inscription naming King Amenemope and Painutem II (priest of Amun no. 124) with a damaged year date has been restored as "Year 53" for Amenemope (Young 1963: 140), and some chronologies have subsequently adopted this higher regnal year (e.g., Green 1983: 390). For Osorkon the Elder, Manetho provides 6 years, and while one inscription of year 2 has been suggested as the highest, Young (1963: 108) notes a year 14, which advocates for an omission of the tens of an original 16 years. While Manetho gives 9 years for Siamun, an inscription for year 17 (Krauss and Warburton 2006: 474) is evidence for the opinion that year 9 should be year 19 (Jansen-Winkeln 2006: 228).

For Psusennes II, Manetho, according to Africanus, provides 14 years for his reign, while Eusebius gives 35 years. However, the Dakhla Stela supplies a year 19, and Krauss (2005: 43–48) has argued for a 24-year reign. With the higher regnal years for Psusennes I, Amenemope, Osorkon, and Psusennes II, dead-reckoning from Ay (Horemheb 15-year reign) results in Shoshenq I ca. 945-924 BC (Table 22).

For the Ramesses II alternative accession of 1333 BC (-16 LD calendar; Horemheb 27-year reign, cf. Krauss 2006: 476–477), the above higher regnal years, except for Osorkon, will result in Shoshenq I ca. 944-923 BC (Table 23).

While the above review of regnal year data uses dead-reckoning between Ramesses II and Shoshenq I, there are three lunar records for the 20th Dynasty and one for the 21st Dynasty (Table 1; cf. Gautschy 2014: 142). However, without a Sothic record many calendar alternatives are possible. If the two lunar records noted by Helck (1964: 153, 162, viz. Ramesses X year 3, II *šmw* 25, LD 1 or 2, and Ramesses XI year 1, III *šmw* 20, NM) are added, the situation is the same. If the possible solar eclipse during the reign of Ramesses V or VI (see below) is added to the lunar records, the number of alternative calendars and chronologies are only slightly reduced.

A -14 FCV chronology based on the above lunar records and solar eclipse will result in Ramesses V 1207-1202 BC, very close to the dead-reckoning chronology (Table 22), but even the conventional calendar (with FCV) has a solution, viz. Ramesses V 1210-1206 BC. So, it appears that additional astronomical records are required to more precisely determine the Egyptian calendar and probable chronology.

Solar Eclipse of Ramesses V

Of note in tomb KV 9 originally cut for Ramesses V, but usurped by VI, is a ceiling mural of two circles overlapping each other by about 85% (Figure 14), which Hentschel (2021: 14) argues may represent a solar eclipse. He assigns the solar eclipse to 11th November, 1143 BC (Ramesses VI ca. 1145-1137 BC), which was 0.81 magn. and 24° alt. at Thebes, but at that altitude it would likely have gone unnoticed. The solar eclipse of 30th October, 1207 BC (Ramesses V ca. 1209-1204 BC), however, was 0.86 magn. and only 9° alt., which would have been detected. The sunset solar eclipse of 16th March, 1186 BC (Ramesses VI ca. 1193-1185 BC) was 0.72 magn., but it did not look like the mural.

Pharaoh's Daughter

In the accounts of the birth of Moses (Exod 1:15–2:9; Acts 7:20-21; Heb 11:23), an edict had been issued sometime previous by a pharaoh to kill male Hebrew[31] infants by casting them into the Nile River to drown, a possible reaction to the Hyksos debacle[32] (Collins 2005: 42). Sometime later Moses was born, and after 3 months his parents could no longer hide him from the authorities, and not being afraid of the pharaoh's edict that male infants must be killed, his mother instead put him in a waterproofed papyrus basket and placed it in the Nile River. A daughter of the ruling pharaoh came down to the Nile to wash and saw the papyrus basket among the reeds. She sent a servant girl to retrieve it, and when she opened it, she found the infant crying.

---

[31] In Exod 1:22 the word Hebrew is present in SP LXX Tg Tg(J) but lacking in MT Vg, possibly from harmonization to Mss lacking the word in v.18. In v.18 4QExod(b) Sa have "Hebrew midwives," but Hebrew is lacking in MT SP LXX Tg Syr Vg, possibly from a one or two-letter homoioteleuton. Alternatively, the addition of Hebrew in vv.18 and 22 could be explication, but context seems to demand at least the addition in v.22.

[32] Collins concluded the decree occurred with an empire pharaoh, possibly Hatshepsut, after Egyptians regained power following the expulsion of the Canaanite Hyksos, in order to prevent another Canaanite takeover of Egypt. Albright (1973: 54; Mahler 1896: 4; Petrovich 2021: 144) believed the king was Ahmose, at the beginning of the 18th Dynasty. Wood (2003: 257–258) argued that the decree first began during the time of Canaanite-Hyksos rule before the beginning of the 18th Dynasty.

Pharaoh's daughter had compassion on him and said, "This is one of the Hebrews' children." She gave the child to his Hebrew mother until she weaned him, and he was then given back to Pharaoh's daughter. An assumption about Pharaoh's daughter is that she was a princess (e.g., Kitchen 2003: 296), and therefore unmarried, and young (Gunn and Fewell 1993: 93), but old enough to care for an infant. The event occurred in the district of Goshen[33] where the Israelite Hebrews had resided since the arrival of Jacob-Israel and his family from Canaan, until the Exodus (Petrovich 2021: 57–167, 215).[34]

Avaris was in the district of Goshen (Kitchen 2003: 261; Petrovich 2021: 125, 198), which had the important naval port of Peru-nefer. Since Moses was 80 when he went before Pharaoh (Exod 7:7) sometime before the Exodus in 1446 BC, his birth would have occurred in 1526 BC. A popular candidate for Pharaoh's daughter based on a High Chronology for Amenhotep II has been Hatshepsut (Haynes 1896: 249; Jack 1925: 251; Finegan 1946: 106; Rea 1961: 10; Petrovich 2021: 147–148).

However, with the High Chronology the age of Hatshepsut in 1526 BC would range from not as yet being

---

[33] The toponym gsm in Papyrus Anastasi IV (1b: 1–2) has been tentatively identified by Groll (1998: 173–192) with the biblical toponym Goshen, which some have equated with LXX Gesem. The Vulgate, translated from a Hebrew text lacking vowels, vocalizes the consonantal Hebrew toponym as Gessen.

[34] Tell el-Dabʿa Phase H Stratum d/2 to Phase C/2 Stratum c.

born, to 7 years.[35] It is believed that Hatshepsut married Thutmose II at the age of 14 or 15 (Bierbrier 1995: 15–19; Tyldesley 1996: 97; Cline 2006: 61), and they had a daughter, Neferurē'. Hatshepsut died in her year 22, when she was between 37 (Nadig 2016: 104) and 50 (Bierbrier 1995: 15–19). In a statue of Princess Neferurē' with her tutor Senenmut, she has her finger on her mouth, symbolizing childhood (Figure 4). The reliefs of Princess Neferurē' in the memorial temple of Hatshepsut at Deir el-Bahari are thought by Laboury (2014: 85) to date to years 5-7.

In the drawing of one relief by Rosellini in ca. 1832 in the Amun-Re section on the South wall of Bark Hall (Figure 6), before the removal of a portion of the relief in the late 19th century (Figures 5 and 7), Princess Neferurē' is depicted as a mostly nude girl with a characteristic side-lock of youth. But on the North wall of Bark Hall (Figure 8) she is dressed as a mature woman in a white robe with ḥtś-scepter, and her head is decorated with a calathos, diadem and, apparently, a royal uraeus (Pawlicki et al. 2007: 113–114; 2017: 21).

Bolshakov (2014: 257) concludes that the adult images of Princess Neferurē' at the memorial temple should be considered fictitious, since he estimates that she would have been only a child. Stela Cairo JdE 38546; Sinai No. 179 from Serabit el-Khadim, with date of year 11, depicts Neferurē' dressed in a long robe and wearing the double feathered crown on a vulture headdress (Figure 9), both usually

---

[35] Her death in 1483 BC + 50 lifespan = 1533 BC birth - 1526 BC. If lifespan 37 years (Nadig 2016: 104), then 1526 BC is six years previous to her birth.

insignia of a queen. The stela may reflect the intention of Hatshepsut for her daughter to succeed her as a queen, or king (Ratié 1972: 231), or perhaps that a marriage occurred by year 11.

In the memorial temple of Hatshepsut at Deir el-Bahari Princess Neferurē' appears in eight separate ritual scenes, although six were later replaced with images of Ahmose and Thutmose I, the parents of Hatshepsut. Pawlicki et al. (2007: 125) suggest that the alterations were done in year 16 as a reaction by Hatshepsut to an unwanted marriage between Princess Neferurē' and Thutmose III. They note that the alterations may be tied to the replacement of the limestone portal with a granite one, which occurred around regnal year 16.

Since there is no mention of Princess Neferurē' in the second tomb of Senenmut (TT 353) at Deir el-Bahari, dated to year 16 of Hatshepsut, it has been suggested that Princess Neferurē' died sometime before year 16. However, stela CG 34013 from the temple of Ptah at Karnak of Thutmose III and his queen Satiah, dated to year 23 or 24, has epigraphical traces in both cartouches of several *nfr* and one R^c signs. It has therefore been argued that, along with the title of *ḥm.t nṯr* "God's Wife," it is likely that the original name in the cartouches was Neferurē' (Pawlicki et al. 2007: 125; Piccione 2003: 93).[36]

---

[36] Pawlicki et al. (2007: 125) note that "Traces of the R^c sign visible in the upper part of the cartouche and then changed to the sign *i'ḥ* constitute secure grounds for reconstructing Neferure's name here originally ..." Piccione (2003: 93) observes that "the bottoms of three *nfr*-signs are distinct in both cartouches. They

The change in the cartouches may have been prompted by the death of Neferurē' sometime after year 23 or 24 of Thutmose III (Piccione 2003: 97; Pawlicki et al. 2007: 124). With consideration of the statues, reliefs, stelae, and other data concerning the age of Princess Neferurē', an age between 2 and 8 in year 1 of Hatshepsut appears a reasonable approximation. If Thutmose IV reigned ca. 1455-1446 BC, dead-reckoning (Table 2) would place the age of Princess Neferurē' at 11 to 17 in 1526 BC at the Moses-Nile incident, year 10 of Hatshepsut. This assumes a 26-year reign for Amenhotep II. The possible alternatives for the reign of Amenhotep II are 30 and 37 years.[37] Using a reign of 37 years for Amenhotep II (accession Hatshepsut 1546 BC), 1526 BC would have been year 21 of Hatshepsut, and the age of Princess Neferurē' between 22 and 28.

For the age range of 2 to 8 years for Princess Neferurē' in year 1 Hatshepsut, the -14 FCV chronology places the age range of Princess Neferurē' at the Moses-Nile event in 1526 BC at between 9 and 15, which would be year 8 Hatshepsut.

---

are plainly evident through the legs and bodies of each duck ... It is clear according to the epigraphical traces in the cartouches, together with the title ḥm.t nṯr, God's Wife, that originally the name Neferure was inscribed on the stela and then subsequently replaced with that of Satiah."

[37] A wine juglet from Amenhotep II's Theban funerary temple reads year 26 which is the highest indisputable regnal date. However, fragmentary papyrus BM 10056 may read either 30 or 35 years for the king. Wente and Van Siclen (1976: 227–228) would infer a reign of 34 years.

For -14 LD, her age range would be 12 to 18, year 11 Hatshepsut.

With the -16 FCV chronology, her age range in 1526 BC would be 20 to 26, year 19 Hatshepsut. For -16 LD, her age would be between 23 to 29, year 22 Hatshepsut. However, the higher ages with -16 calendars may be unlikely if it is posited that Princess Neferurēʿ married around the age of her mother, of no more than 15 when Hatshepsut married Thutmose II (Tyldesley 1996: 97). This is around the time of puberty, viz. between 12 and 15 (Donadoni 1997: 321). As noted above, Pawlicki et al. (2007: 125) proposed that Princess Neferurēʿ married Thutmose III around year 16 of Hatshepsut. In this case, the age of Princess Neferurēʿ in year 16 of Hatshepsut would have been between 17 and 23.

However, if Thutmose III was much younger than Princess Neferurēʿ, e.g., up to around 6 years, then she would have had to wait until he was in puberty. There has been considerable debate about the age of Thutmose III at his accession. It has often been suggested that he was around age 2 (e.g., O'Connor 2006: 23), though Harris and Wente (1980: 247) propose an age between 2 and 13, and Matić (2016: 813) suggests age 9, while von Beckerath (1994: 112) recommends age 5 or 6.

As discussed above, if the title "Pharaoh's daughter" indicates an unmarried young princess, capable of raising a child, and her mother Hatshepsut was married sometime in the range of puberty, we would also expect Princess Neferurēʿ to marry at puberty. Therefore, the -14 calendars, which put her age between either 9 to 15 or 12 to 18, are favored. Laboury (2014: 85) believed the reliefs of Princess

Neferurē' with her sidelock of youth in the memorial temple of Hatshepsut at Deir el-Bahari date to years 5 to 7. With her age between 2 and 8 in year 1 Hatshepsut, she would have been between 6 and 14, where 10 to 14 would seem more likely.

The -14 calendars place the Moses-Nile incident in 1526 BC between years 8 and 11 of Hatshepsut. Year 11 is the date inscribed on Stela Cairo JdE 38546, which depicts Neferurē' dressed as a queen. JdE 38546 may be evidence that she was married in or by year 11 of Hatshepsut, with her age range 12 to 18, although the relief on the Stela could be simply propaganda.

If Neferurē' needed to hide the origin of Moses from Thutmose III, it may seem probable that she would have been unmarried at the Moses-Nile event, and therefore in the early range of puberty. However, hiding the origins of Moses may not have been a concern. Hoffmeier (1996: 147) writes that "Thutmose III… initiated the practice of bringing the princes of subject kings of western Asia to Egypt to be trained in Egyptian ways so as to prepare them to replace their fathers upon their death," and Janzen (2023: 21) notes, "Some local rulers, no doubt familiar with this Egyptian policy, even sent their sons to be raised in Egypt in order to show their loyalty."

An indication that it was known in the royal court that Pharaoh's daughter had adopted Moses, and that this was not a problem, is that he was known as "the son of Pharaoh's daughter" (Heb 11:24), though his origin as a Hebrew that had been spared a death in the Nile River, contrary to Egyptian law, may have been kept secret. This would have required the female servants of Pharaoh's daughter to have taken an oath of secrecy.

Concerning the identity of the Pharaoh who gave the command to drown Hebrew infants by throwing them into the Nile, the verbs in the biblical text point to a male Pharaoh, which eliminates Hatshepsut.[38] However, the text suggests that this law had been in effect for some time (Exod 1:17–22), and probably followed closely after the expulsion of the Hyksos, so pharaohs from Ahmose to Thutmose II are likely candidates. Petrovich (2021:144–147; Haynes 1896: 249) opted for Thutmose I, who may be a good candidate.

It is probable that the 13-acre palatial complex at Avaris, modern 'Ezbet Helmy, that was built on the eastern bank of the Pelusiac branch of the Nile (Figures 10 and 11), was constructed during the joint reign of Hatshepsut and Thutmose III (Morgan 2004: 285; Bietak and Forstner -Müller 2011: 29; Bietak 2018: 85–86). The size of the largest palace and the precinct suggests that it was likely the residence of a member of the royal family, if not the king himself (Forstner-Müller 2011: 29).

The palace precinct was likely a copy of the royal residence at Memphis (Bietak 2010: 23). Palace G at Avaris was one of the largest in Egypt, and it contained the largest throne room found in Egypt. Palaces F and G were decorated with Minoan frescoes (Figure 12). A newly built palatial complex in the district of Goshen was apparently the reason why Pharaoh's daughter was residing there at the time

---

[38] Collins (2005: 42) held the possibility that it could have been Hatshepsut.

Moses was born. The ruling Pharaoh, her mother Hatshepsut, had been building a palatial complex there which had several palaces (F, G and J), and it is therefore likely that Princess Neferurē' stayed at one of the palaces when Hatshepsut resided at Avaris.

An alternative chronology (Table 6) was examined based on the earliest possible Sothic solutions in order to allow the possibility that both Amenhotep II and Thutmose IV celebrated year 34 *Heb sed* renewal festivals. This chronology moves the accessions of Hatshepsut and Thutmose III earlier to 1558 BC. Thutmose III was likely between 2 and 6 years old at accession. If he married Neferurē' or Satiah at 14, the maximum age of a daughter at the Moses-Nile incident in 1526 BC would be 23. However, the only known daughters of Thutmose III are from his later royal wife Merytre-Hatshepsut. In addition, the lack of ceramic evidence for Thutmose IV at Tell el-Dab'a is inexplicable if he had a 34-year reign, while the indirect evidence is that his reign was likely short.

A remaining question concerns the alternative of Amenhotep II, 1475-1446 BC, based on an Egyptian calendar of -11 and FCV (Table 17). The estimated lifespan for Hatshepsut, according to Nadig (2016: 104), is 37 to 47, with a consensus being 47, while Bierbrier (1995: 15–19) suggests a maximum age of 50. For a maximum age of 37, Hatshepsut would have been age 15 in 1526 BC at the Moses-Nile event, making her seem a good candidate for Pharaoh's daughter based on the above assumptions. However, Hatshepsut would have been married to Thutmose II in or by 1526 BC. For the consensus age of 47, she would have been queen, and the next year, she would be Coregent/Pharaoh. This is a peculiar scenario for one who was called "Pharaoh's daughter," and at the Moses-Nile incident dated 1526 BC, in this scenario, Hatshepsut would have already had a child, Neferurēʻ.

Summary and Conclusion

This study tested the theory of Collins that Thutmose IV may have been the Pharaoh of the Exodus. Based on biblical and extra-biblical chronological data, the most probable date for the Exodus is 1446 BC. The extant records for the reign of Thutmose IV suggest a reign of 8-10 years, which places Thutmose IV ca. 1455-1446 BC. This is 55 years earlier than the Low Chronology of 1401-1391 BC for his reign. These theories were tested with astronomical records (Sothic, lunar, solar eclipse, solar alignment), archaeology, and additional historical records.

The prevalent suggestion that Ramesses II is a candidate for the Exodus Pharaoh is based primarily on the toponym of Ramesses in Exod 1:11, a city which was built during the Israelite oppression. Among the problems with this assignment are the historical records. Notably, this pharaoh would have survived the Yam Suph incident, contrary to Exod 14:17 and Ps 136:15, and then he would have continued the might of Egypt during the Israelite wilderness sojourn and the Israelite Conquest, at a time when the book of Joshua lacks mention of an encounter with Egyptian troops.

Further, the Berlin Pedestal, dated to the reign of Ramesses II, mentions a people in Canaan known as "Israel." If the Exodus is placed in his mid-reign, he still would have escaped the Yam Suph event, and the Conquest would have begun toward the end of Merneptah's reign, but the Merneptah Stele also mentions Israel in Canaan. Placing the Exodus at the last year of Ramesses II seems to solve the Yam Suph problem, but results in the Conquest occurring in the reign of Ramesses III, who had campaigns into the Levant as far as Byblos and apparently into Syria.

In addition, the chronological data in 1 Kgs 6:1 of 4th Solomon plus 479 years to the Exodus, the Jubilee Years arriving at the same Exodus date, the 300 years of Judg 11:26, and the genealogy in 1 Chr 6:33–37 result in a host of problems for a late-date (13th cent.) Exodus/Conquest Model. Thus, in consideration of just the above problems, Ramesses II is a poor candidate.

A prevalent suggestion for the early date (15th cent.) Exodus/Conquest Model is Amenhotep II. This theory began with a conventional Egyptian High Chronology, which somewhat overlaps Amenhotep II with the Exodus date of 1446 BC. However, this theory results in Amenhotep II surviving the Yam Suph incident, and only 7 months later, he would have resumed significant military activity in the Levant with an army strong enough to take captive about 100,000 Asiatics, contrary to expectations of an Egypt in ruin following the plagues. According to Deut 11:4, option 3, Egypt did not fully recover for at least 40 years. The historical evidence does not favor Amenhotep II as a candidate.

Thutmose III is an apparent candidate with the Low Chronology, which overlaps 1446 BC, but this also results in the pharaoh escaping the Yam Suph event mid-career, and then his military campaigns into Asia would have continued unabated, contrary to the evidence that the Israelites did not encounter Egyptian resistance during the Conquest, which they surely would have encountered if Thutmose III was still in power.

At Tell el-Dab'a a stratum marks a Hiatus, which occurred after the reign of Amenhotep II or Thutmose IV. The workshops of the slaves were abandoned, leaving their work behind. This is compatible with the biblical Exodus account. The abandonment is approximately Late Bronze IA/LB IB. The High Chronology for Amenhotep II puts the Exodus of 1446 BC in the pharaoh's year 7, which is contrary to the archaeology that the site was abandoned *after* Amenhotep II. Moving Amenhotep II terminus to 1446 BC solves the problem. Later in LB IB in Canaan, conflagrations destroyed Jericho (City IV(c) or V(a)), Ai (Khirbet el-Maqatir), and Hazor (Stratum XV, and Stratum 2). Evidence was found at Khirbet el-Maqatir and Hazor that the conquerors decapitated figurines. Smashing idols was a biblical command. The archaeological data is consistent with the biblical Conquest of Canaan, and the above archaeological data provides a reasonable test for Exodus Pharaoh candidates.

To further test the hypothesis that Thutmose IV reigned ca. 55 years earlier than currently believed, astronomical records contemporary with the 18th Dynasty were examined to evaluate if such a move earlier is possible. With the hypothesis that Thutmose IV reigned ca. 1455-1446 BC, the Sirius heliacal rising information in the Ebers and Khnum records were found to suggest that the conventional Egyptian calendar is off by +14 to +18 days. The lunar data was then tested with Egyptian calendars adjusted from -14 days to -18 days.

Two methods for calculating lunar day 1 for the Egyptian calendar, viz. first evening crescent visibility (FCV) and first dawn of old crescent invisibility (LD), were used for -14, -16 and -18[39] calendars. From the lunar match results (Table 24), -14 FCV, -14 LD and -16 FCV have equivalent fits to the data, the exception being -16 LD,[40] though it is still a possible solution. Since the overall lunar match results between the calendars are not markedly different, it could be concluded that neither the results nor the sample size are sufficient to answer the question of whether the 18th Dynasty was using FCV or LD for the start of the lunar month.

Two solutions for the year 21 lunar record of Amenhotep III are 1426 BC (-14 FCV and -16 LD), accession 1446 BC, and 1423 BC (-16 FCV), accession 1443 BC. The years 1446 BC or 1443 BC are possible candidates for the last year of Thutmose IV and the accession of Amenhotep III. Gedge (2022) calculated Solomon's 4th year at 964 BC. Adding 479 years (instead of his 480) results in an Exodus date of 1443 BC.[41]

---

[39] Data not shown for -18.

[40] A preliminary analysis of 40 12th Dynasty lunar dates using different Egyptian calendars in a 75-year range also found that the best fit occurred with a calendar using either -14 FCV or -16 LD. Cf. appendix.

[41] The chronology of Hayes and Hooker date the end of Solomon's reign to 926 BC. Projecting earlier, Solomon's 4th

Date	-14 FCV	-16 FCV	-14 LD	-16 LD
I *šmw* 21	-1	0	0	0
II *prt* 30	0	0	0	-1
III *šmw* 15	0	0	0	-2
III *šmw* 11	0	0	0	-1
II *šmw* 30	0	0	0	-2
III *šmw* 1	0	0	+1	0
II *prt* 27	+1/0	-1	0	0

Table 24: Summary of lunar match results with different Egyptian calendars and observation methods.

An alternate solution based on the year 21 lunar record of Amenhotep III suggests a possible reign for an unattested regent of 1449-1446 BC (-14 LD). However, there is no historical evidence for an unattested regent.

If the last year of Amenhotep II is placed at 1446 BC, Sothic and lunar solutions are possible. The result is a reign from 1475 to 1446 BC based on a -11 calendar with FCV. His reign would be no more than 29 years.[42] As noted above, another remaining problem with Amenhotep II's candidature is that Thutmose IV would have reasserted Egyptian power at a time when the expectation following the

---

year would be ca. 963/62 BC, with Exodus ca. 1442/41 BC. Their chronology has several emendations, e.g., Baasha's 24 years to 22 years, Asa's 41 years to 29 years, Ahab's 22 years to 15 years, and Jehu's 28 years to 18 years.

[42] The High Chronology of Petrovich (2006: 91–93; 2021: 27–28) assumes a 37-year reign, apparently based on arguments by Wente and Van Siclen, though the latter prefer a 34-year reign (1976: 218, 227–229).

plagues and Yam Suph incident is that Egypt would be in severe ruin.

The recently joined tablet fragments KUB 19.15+KBo 50.24 have a synchronism of year 8/9 of Muršili II with the accession of Pharaoh Ay. The Hittite solar omen record in year 9/10 of the Annals of Muršili II, therefore, provides a means to establish an absolute date for Pharaoh Ay. The preferred time for the military campaign noted in year 9/10 of the Annals is spring. The only spring solar eclipse that would likely have been observed between 1392-1290 BC is the 0.96-0.99 magnitude eclipse of 3rd May, 1375 BC. The absolute date for the accession of Ay is therefore 1376 BC.

A suitable candidate for this solar eclipse record has been elusive to researchers, but occurs ca. 53 years earlier than the Low Chronology for the accession of Ay. Dead-reckoning of the reigns of the Pharaohs from year 1 of Ay results in Thutmose IV ca. 1455-1446 BC. The eclipse of 3rd May, 1375 BC is also possible for candidate Amenhotep II, ca. 1475-1446 BC, if there was a coregency between Amenhotep III and Akhenaten.

Astronomical alignments can be calculated from the date inscriptions on the Boundary Stelae at Akhenaten's city of Akhetaten. The date of IV *prt* 13 on 5th March has solutions that support the conventional calendar with the Low Chronology, and -14 calendars (based on Thutmose IV 1455-1446 BC), but the High Chronology (1370-1353 BC), -16 calendars (based on Thutmose IV alternative), and -11 calendars (based on Amenhotep II 1475-1446 BC) have no solution for 5th March, unless the observation date is moved. For the theory of an unattested coregent (Table 4), one would have to posit a reign of 40 years for Amenhotep III (1449-1409/8 BC), which is marginal or unlikely.

Several Amarna Letters describe a conquest of Canaan by the 'Apîru/Ḫabiru *en masse*. A number of scholars believe the evidence suggests that some of the 'Apîru/Ḫabiru' are the Israelite-Hebrews. A biblical year for the Israelite Conquest of Canaan is 1406 BC, and the end of Joshua's military activity occurred sometime in 1400 BC, though some tribes continued military activity into the Judges period. With Thutmose IV ca. 1455-1446 BC, the -14 (FCV and LD) and -16 (LD) calendar chronologies place the accession of Akhenaten in ca. 1408 BC, while Amenhotep II ca. 1475-1446 would date Akhenaten accession to either ca. 1408 BC or 1400 BC. Letter EA 254 can be dated to either year 12 (Akhenaten) or year 32 (Amenhotep III).

For Akhenaten accession 1408 BC or 1400 BC, EA 254 year 12 is 1397 BC or 1389 BC, respectively. Both of these dates are reasonable. The possible reading of year 32 (Amenhotep III) for EA 254 is less favorable, placing EA 254 before Abib/Nisan 1406 BC. The EA 254 synchronism, like Tell el-Dab'a, is not specific enough to decide between Thutmose IV and Amenhotep II as the Exodus Pharaoh.

With the movement of Thutmose IV to ca. 1455-1446 BC, a new candidate for the identity of "Pharaoh's daughter" (Exod 2:5) emerges, who rescued the infant Moses from the Nile River. The expectation of Pharaoh's daughter is that she was a princess, unmarried and young, but old enough to care for an infant. Princess Neferurēʿ was the daughter of Pharaoh Thutmose II and Hatshepsut. Since her mother Hatshepsut married around age 15, which is in the range of puberty (abouyt 12-15), it would be assumed that Princess Neferurē' would marry in a similar age range.

The -16 chronologies suggest her age at either 20 to 26 (-16 FCV) or 23 to 29 (-16 LD). Her age, with dead reckoning of the reigns of the pharaoh's, would be 11 to 17. The -14 chronologies result in her age at either 9 to 15 (-14 FCV) or 12 to 18 (-14 LD) at the Moses-Nile event in 1526 BC. While the -16 chronologies cannot be ruled out, the -14 and dead-reckoning chronologies match the expected age range for puberty of about 12 to 15. Overall, the -14 FCV calendar and chronology has the best fit of the data.

While many problems with candidate Amenhotep II occur using the High Chronology, several were solved by moving the terminus of the pharaoh to 1446 BC, based on a -11 FCV calendar. The remaining problems are, 1) the power of Egypt would have continued with Thutmose IV following the plagues and the Yam Suph event, 2) no solar eclipse candidate for KUB 14.4, unless a questionable coregency of 8 or 9 years is placed between Amenhotep III and Akhenaten, 3) a poor solution for the solar alignment dates on the Boundary Stelae at Akhetaten, and 4) no reasonable candidate for Pharaoh's daughter, unless the lifespan for Hatshepsut is reduced from the consensus of 47 years to 37.

The study by Collins moving Thutmose IV ca. 55 years earlier than the Low Chronology was found to be supported by, 1) the solar eclipse candidate for year 9/10 of Muršili II (on 3rd May, 1375 BC; year 2 Pharaoh Ay; KUB 14.4 and KUB 19.15+KBo 50.24), 2) the contemporary Egyptian Sothic and lunar records (Amenhotep I, Thutmose III,

Amenhotep II, Amenhotep III and Ramesses II; -14 or -16 calendar chronologies), 3) the solar alignment solutions based on the dates for years 5 and 6 on the Akhetaten Boundary Stelae (-14 or -16 calendar chronologies), 4) the Stratum-b/c (LB IA/LB IB) abandonment at Tell el-Dab'a (terminus Amenhotep II or Thutmose IV), and 5) a candidate for Pharaoh's daughter (Exod 2:5; Princess Neferurē'; -14 calendar chronologies).

The movement of Thutmose IV ca. 55 years earlier than the Low Chronology[43] therefore finds an array of additional support.

---

[43] Collins (2005: 67) concludes, "Compared to the middle and low chronologies, an upward adjustment of 55 to 60 years would be necessary. Although many scholars wince at such adjustments, most realize that the chronological uncertainties inherent in Egyptian documents could, if necessary, accommodate such a revision."

Appendix: The Sothic Cycle

Introduction

The ancient Egyptian civil calendar is thought to have been introduced in the early third millennium BC. It began with an observation of the heliacal rising of Sirius (spdt or Sopdet; Greek Sothis) on the first day of the month of Akhet. The heliacal rising of Sirius is the first time the star is visible after a period of invisibility of lasting about 70 days at Memphis.

The Egyptian civil calendar was divided into three seasons of Akhet (*3ḥt*), Peret (*prt*) and Shemu (*šmw*). Each season contains four months of 30 days, with five additional days at the end. While the Egyptian year was 365 days, a heliacal rising of Sirius occurs at the same location every 365 ¼ days, so the start of the Egyptian year progressively moved one day earlier every four years in comparison to the stars and the Julian calendar. The Sirius rising will occur again on the Egyptian New Year (I *3ḥt* 1) after approximately 1460 Julian years or 1461 Egyptian years, a Sothic cycle.

The Sothic cycle hypothesis most similar to current theory was initially formulated by Meyer in *Agyptische Chronologie* (1904). Meyer found six Sothic records, on which much of current Egyptian chronology is based. This relies on the assumption that the Roman author Censorinus (ca. 238 AD) gave accurate information of a heliacal rising of Sirius that occurred 100 years previous on the Egyptian New Year, retrocalculated as 20th July, 139 AD. If this date is correct, and the Egyptian calendar was not modified since its inception in the third Millenium, any document including both a Sothic observation and a civil date can be assigned a date within a 4 year period, which can frequently be refined by a lunar date to a specific year.

However, there have been a number of criticisms levelled against the reliability of Sothic cycle dating, viz. the veracity of Censorinus' information, unknown latitude of the observation of Sirius, lack of a name of the pharaoh, the absence of a regnal date on the observation, and whether the civil calendar remained unchanged. However, it is here assumed that the consensus on the reliability of Sothic dating is likely.

New Kingdom

The heliacal Sirius rising date on the Ebers papyrus of year 9 on III Shemu 9 is thought to belong to the reign of Amenhotep I. A second New Kingdom Sothic record is attributed to Thutmose III on III Shemu 28 and at least three quarters of a century later.

As noted in the study, the joined tablet fragments KUB 19.15+KBo 50.24 have a synchronism of year 8/9 of Muršili II with the accession of Pharaoh Ay. Muršili II recorded a solar omen in his year 9/10 during a military march (KUB 14.4). If this apparent solar eclipse occurred in spring, the only spring solar eclipse that would have likely been observed in the period 1390-1290 BC was the solar eclipse of 3rd May, 1375 BC, 0.96-0.99 magnitude. This places Ay ca. 53 years earlier than the Low Chronology, and the Sothic and lunar records subsequently only have solutions if the conventional reconstructed Egyptian calendar is corrected by subtracting 14 to 16 days when comparing with the Julian Calendar. As will be seen below, this -14 or -16 reconstructed calendar was probably also in use during the reign of Senusret III of the 12th Dynasty.

There is a question as to what observation method was being used for the beginning of the lunar month. The consensus has been to accept first dawn of old crescent invisibility (LD), while others have suggested first evening crescent visibility (FCV). For Amenhotep I and Thutmose III, calculations for the Sothic and lunar records were performed for -14 LD, -14 FCV, -16 LD and -16 FCV. For observation at Elephantine, accession dates for Amenhotep I and Thutmose III for -14 LD are Amenhotep I 1582 BC, and Thutmose III 1536 BC. For -14 FCV, accession Amenhotep I is 1582 BC, and Thutmose III 1533 BC.

For -16 LD, accession Amenhotep I is 1593 BC, and accession Thutmose III is 1547 BC. For -16 FCV, Amenhotep I accession is 1590 BC, and Thutmose III is 1544 BC. In comparison, for the conventional calendar (0 LD) and observation at Thebes, Amenhotep I accession is 1526 BC. If observation at Memphis or Heliopolis, the accession would be 1545 BC. For Thutmose III, accession is either 1479 BC (Low Chronology) or 1504 BC (High Chronology).

Middle Kingdom

If the above dates for the New Kingdom are approximately 55 years earlier than the Low Chronology, it is probable that the Middle Kingdom dates should be raised by a similar amount. Berlin papyrus 10012 is usually attributed to Senusret III, but could be Amenemhat III, and reads,

You should know that the going forth of Sopdet [Sirius] takes place on the 16th day of the 8th month.....

It is believed that this is a prediction of the heliacal rising of the star Sirius on IV Peret 16. Some 40 lunar dates are attached to priest duty periods or religious festival dates recorded on the Berlin papyri (Luft 1992). These have been used for dating of the Egyptian 12th Dynasty, particularly the reigns of Senusret III and Amenemhat III, which are conventionally dated to no later than 1837-1796 BC and 1818-1773 BC, respectively (Krauss 2007).

Solutions to date the heliacal rising on IV Peret 16 in year 7 have proposed observations of the event from Memphis (Parker 1970; 1977; Luft 1992). It has also been proposed that the Sothic date be raised to IV Peret 18 and that the heliacal rising of Sirius was observed at Elephantine (Krauss 1985; 2007), which would fit the dates given above.

In the early 2nd Millenium BC, the heliacal rising of Sirius occurred between 10th July at Elephantine to 17th July at Memphis. This suggests a 31-year window, with a fixed 365-day Egyptian calendar. A set of 12 consecutive dates from year 30-31 on Berlin 102056A verso or D and 2 dates in year 32 on Berlin 10006 or C of Amenemhat III help to limit the search area. There are two search sequences based on interpretation of the lunar sequence in year 30-31 on D (Parker 1977).

Papyrus		Egypt	Julian		FCV date	Date
	Yr	Date	-14		-14	BC
10092	5	II.24	22-Jan	=	22-Jan	1911
10009	5	VI.22	20-May	=	20-May	1911
10282 (1)	6	I.14	13-Dec	=	13-Dec	1911
10282 (2)	6	II.13	11-Jan	=	11-Jan	1910
10282 (3)	6	III.13	10-Feb	=	10-Feb	1910
10012	7	VIII.16	12-Jul			1909
10130 (1)	8	II.21	18-Jan	=	18-Jan	1908
10130 (2)	8	III.21	17-Feb	=	17-Feb	1908
10003 (E)	9	VII.9	5-Jun	1	4-Jun	1907
10112	10	IV.29	27-Mar	=	27-Mar	1906
10412	11	I.20	18-Dec	=	18-Dec	1906
10165	12	X.5	29-Aug	1	28-Aug	1904
10248 (F)	14	II.17	13-Jan	=	13-Jan	1902
10011	16	VI.23	18-May	=	18-May	1900
10016 (G)	18	IX.30	23-Aug	=	23-Aug	1898
*Near misses		0	Mismatch or		2 of 14 2 of 14	

Table 1. Lunar dates of Senusret III year 1 =1915 BC -14 day
calendar shift first crescent visibilities (FCV).

Results

After undertaking a search, a number of potential year 30
candidates were found: that would put the accession of
Amenemhat III in 1935, 1932, 1924, 1910 1899, 1895 1893,
1888, 1882, 1877, 1872, 1869, 1867, 1865 and 1861 BC
respectively, and Senusret III 19 years earlier than the dates
listed. Those lunar sequences that failed to match less than 8
dates (also counting near misses as hits) out of the 12 dates
were excluded from further analysis.

The most promising dates were compared with the complete set of dates (Tables 1-4).

Papyrus		Egypt	Julian		LD date	Date
	Yr	Date	-16		-16	BC
10092	5	II.24	20-Jan	1	21-Jan*	1911
10009	5	VI.22	18-May		19-May	1911
10282 (1)	6	I.14	11-Dec	=	11-Dec	1911
10282 (2)	6	II.13	9-Jan	=	9-Jan	1910
10282 (3)	6	III.13	8-Feb	=	8-Feb	1910
10012	7	VIII.16	10-Jul			1909
10130 (1)	8	II.21	16-Jan	=	16-Jan	1909
10130 (2)	8	III.21	15-Feb	=	15-Feb	1908
10003 (E)	9	VII.9	3-Jun	=	3-Jun	1907
10112	10	IV.29	25-Mar	=	25-Mar	1906
10412	11	I.20	16-Dec	1	17-Dec*	1906
10165	12	X.5	27-Aug	=	27-Aug	1904
10248 (F)	14	II.17	11-Jan	=	11-Jan	1902
10011	16	VI.23	16-May	1	17-May	1900
10016 (G)	18	IX.30	21-Aug	=	21-Aug	1898
*Near misses		0	Mismatch		3 of 14	
			or		1 of 14	

Table 2. Lunar dates of Senusret III year 1 =1915 BC -16 day calendar shift Lunar disappearances (LD).

| Papyrus | | Egypt | Julian | | FCV date | Date |
	Yr	Date	-14		-14	BC
10090 (A)	3	XI.16	7-Oct	=	7-Oct	1894
10056 (1)	8	III.26	18-Feb	=	18-Feb	1889
10056 (2)	8	IV.26	19-Mar	=	19-Mar	1889
10166	9	II.16	8-Jan	=	8-Jan	1888
c58065 (H)	9	X.12	1-Sep	=	1-Sep	1888
10018	10	II.5	28-Dec	1	29-Dec	1888
10079	10	III.5	27-Jan	=	27-Jan	1887
10344	11	III.24	15-Feb	=	15-Feb	1886
10052	24	I.5	25-Nov	1	24-Nov	1874
10104	24	VII.2	20-May	=	20-May	1873
10062 (B)	29	IX.7	20-Sep	=	19-Sep	1868
10056 (D1)	30	X.25	9-Sep	1	8-Sep*	1867
10056 (D2)	30	XI.24	8-Oct-	=	8-Oct	1867
10056 (D3)	30	XII.24	7-Nov	=	7-Nov	1867
10056 (D4)	31	I.18	6-Dec	1	7-Dec	1867
10056 (D5)	31	II.18	5-Jan	=	5-Jan	1866
10056 (D6)	31	III.18	4-Feb-	=	4-Feb-	1866
10056 (D7)	31	IV.18	6-Mar	1	5-Mar*	1866
10056 (D8)	31	V.17	4-Apr	=	4-Apr	1866
10056 (D9)	31	VI.17	4-May	=	4-May	1866
10056 (D10)	31	VII.16	2-Jun-24	=	2-Jun-24	1866
10056 (D11)	31	VIII.16	2-Jul	1	1-Jul	1866
10056 (D12)	31	IX.15	31-Jul	=	31-Jul	1866
10006 (C1)	32	II.8	26-Dec	=	26-Dec	1866
10006 (C2)	32	III.7	24-Jan	=	24-Jan	1865
10206	36	II.24	10-Jan	=	10-Jan	1861
*Near miss			Mismatch		6 of 26	
			or		5 of 26	

Table 3. Lunar dates of Amenemhat III year 1 = 1896 BC -14
day calendar shift first crescent visibilities (FCV).

Papyrus	Yr	Egypt Date	Julian -16		LD date -16	Date BC
10090 (A)	3	XI.16	5-Oct	=	5-Oct	1894
10056 (1)	8	III.26	16-Feb	=	16-Feb	1889
10056 (2)	8	IV.26	17-Mar	1	16-Mar	1889
10166	9	II.16	6-Jan	=	6-Jan	1888
c58065 (H)	9	X.12	30-Aug	=	30-Aug	1888
10018	10	II.5	26-Dec	1	27-Dec	1888
10079	10	III.5	25-Jan	=	25-Jan	1887
10344	11	III.24	13-Feb	=	13-Feb	1886
10052	24	I.5	23-Nov	=	23-Nov	1874
10104	24	VII.2	18-May	1	17-May	1873
10062 (B)	29	IX.7	18-Sep	1	17-Sep	1868
10056 (D1)	30	X.25	7-Sep	=	7-Sep	1867
10056 (D2)	30	XI.24	6-Oct	=	6-Oct	1867
10056 (D3)	30	XII.24	5-Nov	=	5-Nov	1867
10056 (D4)	31	I.18	4-Dec	=	4-Dec	1867
10056 (D5)	31	II.18	3-Jan	=	3-Jan	1866
10056 (D6)	31	III.18	2-Feb	1	1-Feb*	1866
10056 (D7)	31	IV.18	4-Mar	=	4-Mar	1866
10056 (D8)	31	V.17	2-Apr	=	2-Apr	1866
10056 (D9)	31	VI.17	2-May	=	2-May	1866
10056 (D10)	31	VII.16	31-May	=	31-May	1866
10056 (D11)	31	VIII.16	30-Jun	=	30-Jun	1866
10056 (D12)	31	IX.15	29-Jul	=	29-Jul	1866
10006 (C1)	32	II.8	24-Dec	=	24-Dec	1866
10006 (C2)	32	III.7	22-Jan	=	22-Jan	1865
10206	36	II.24	8-Jan	=	8-Jan	1861
*Near miss			Mismatch		5 of 26	
			or		4 of 26	

Table 4. Lunar dates of Amenemhat III year 1 = 1896 BC -16 day calendar shift Lunar disappearances (LD).

Discussion

In the analysis by Luft (1992) of 39 of the 40 available dates the best result was obtained with Amenemhat III year 30 = 1824 BC, but there were at least 14 misses out of the 39 dates analyzed (error 35.8%). This current analysis has a lower error rate than for the traditional dates of Luft (1992). The lowest error rate was found for LD -16 days and then for FCV -14 days out of step with the traditional Egyptian calendar, each with 8 misses from 40 lunar dates, an error rate of 20%. However, each sequence had 3 (LD) and 2 (FCV) near misses, respectively, potentially reducing the error rate to 12.5% and 15%.

There was no satisfactory match with -14 LD or -16 FCV reductions of the Egyptian calendar in the mid to early 19th and late 20th Century BC. Lunar sequences corresponding to these criteria had between 55% and 65% mismatches with the predicted lunar phases. However, -17 LD and -15 FCV calendar reductions 29 years earlier achieved matches with 75% of the lunar dates.

Overall, Amenemhat III year 30 = 1867 BC gave the best result, and lunar disappearance supported the heliacal rising of Sirius on the 10th July, 1909 BC (Senusret III year 7 at Elephantine), with a -16 day calendar shift. Amenemhat III year 30 = 1867 BC also gave the best result with FCV, and had the lowest error. It required observation of the heliacal rising of Sirius on 12th July, 1909 BC (Senusret III year 7, and presumably at Thebes), which required a 14-day calendar shift. Both of these sequences date Senusret III year 1 in 1915 BC and Amenemhat III year 1 in 1896 BC. A -14 day or -16 day calendar shift thus appears to be confirmed by this analysis of 12th Dynasty lunar dates, in line with the above analysis of the lunar dates of the New Kingdom. [44]

Historical Synchronisms

The above -14 or -16 days calendar chronologies move Senusret III ca. 40 years earlier, and this may be supported by historical synchronisms. Senusret III instituted great administrative reforms, including a new governmental system organizing three main administrative divisions with departments in the north, south, and one of the head of the south (Mieroop 2011: 106). Approximately in the second half of his reign the provincial governors (or nomarchs) were stripped of their traditional rights and privileges (Hayes 1971: 505–506; Shaw and Nicholson 1995: 259; Melandri 2011: 249–270).

Several scholars have placed Joseph during Senusret III (Payne 1954: 47; Wood 1970: 114). Battenfield (1972: 83) believes the reduction of the power of the nomarchs during Senusret III was the result of the administrative duties of the vizier Joseph in preparation for the 7 years of plenty and or the events during the 7 years of famine (Gen 41:34-36, 47-49, 54-56; 47:14-26). Joseph began the office of vizier (Gen 41:40) in 1886 BC (Finegan 1998: 207; Steinmann 2011: 79).[45]

---

[44] This section for the Middle Kingdom is condensed from the forthcoming article by D. F. Lappin.

[45] Joseph was made ruler over all the land of Egypt (Gen 41:41). Chronologies that posit Joseph in the 17th century BC based on a 215-year sojourn in Egypt (Exod 12:40 LXX), instead of a 430-

-14 FCV or -16 LD:

Amenemhat II	1956-1921 BC
Senusret II	1924-1915 BC
Senusret III	1915-1876 BC
Amenemhat III	1896-1851 BC

Conventional Chronology:

Amenemhat II	1919-1884 BC
Senusret II	1887-1878 BC
Senusret III	1878-1840 BC
Amenemhat III	1859-1813 BC

Joseph's Chronology:

Accession as vizier	1886 BC
7 years of plenty	1886-1879 BC
7 years of famine	1879-1872 BC
Jacob to Egypt	1876 BC

During the reign of Amenemhat III the Middle Kingdom attained its cultural and economic zenith. The King implemented significant agricultural plans which reclaimed large areas for cultivation by manipulating the water level of

---

year sojourn (MT), place Joseph during the Hyksos Period. However, his rule as vizier could not have happened during the Hyksos era, since the Hyksos never ruled over all the land of Egypt, but only controlled the delta region. Further, native Egyptians were concerned about personal cleanliness and the removal of facial hair, while the Hyksos were not. Before going before pharaoh, Joseph had to change clothes and shave (Gen 41:14; Ailing (2002: 23)).

the Fayum Lake, known by the Greeks as Lake Moeris[46] (now Lake Qarun).

The Fayum is a region in a depression that water flowed into whenever the Nile overflowed. Under Amenemhat III the waterway from the Nile to Lake Moeris was widened and deepened. This was done to control the Nile flood, regulate the water level during dry seasons, and provide water in the surrounding area for land reclamation (Ibrahim 2019: 29–46).

The system which regulated the inflow of water into Lake Moeris reclaimed thousands of acres of land for agricultural use. This waterway branched off the Nile at Assiut, flowing parallel to the Nile for over 200 kilometers until it reached Lahun, where after a short distance the waterway then discharged into Lake Moeris.

The 12th Dynasty name for the waterway is unknown, though there were several names for it attested in papyri. In Greek it was known as the Great Canal,[47] Argaitis Canal, and Tomis River.[48] In Demotic it was called *t3 ḥn.t n Mr-wr*, "the canal of Moeris" (Kraemer 2010: 367). The Arabic name for the waterway is the Bahr Yussef, "waterway of Joseph."

---

[46] The Greeks considered Amenemhat III the king responsible for the waterway, and called him "King Moeris." Cf. Wendrich and Holdaway (2017: 1).

[47] A possible translation of Egyptian *Mr-wr*, or "Great Waterway." Cf. Morgan (2023).

[48] Perhaps a derivation from Egyptian *t3-ʿm*, "the channel." Haug (2024: 43 and n. 22).

Thus, the administrative reforms and loss of the power of the provincial governors during Senusret III, and the great agricultural projects and economic zenith during Amenemhat III, reflect a period very similar to what would be expected from some of the activites of the vizier Joseph described in Gen 41 and 47. With the conventional chronology, however, Joseph would not have been vizier during Amenemhat III, but rather during Senusret II and Senusret III.

Old Kingdom

There are a few dates of interest for the Old Kingdom. An inscription on an ancient Egyptian ointment jar, stylistically dated to mid to late 5th Dynasty, records a heliacal rising of Sirius (Gautschy et al. 2017b: 71). It reads:

Ointment for the protection of the year, month 4, Peret-season, for the forthcoming of Sopdet [Sothis], month 4, Akhet-season it is, made for the first day of the month.

Gautschy et al. have accession of Khufu as either 2503 BC (Low Chronology) or 2636 BC (High Chronology). With Senusret III accession at 1915 BC, we would expect an accession date for Khufu very close to the High Chronology date of Gautschy et al. This movement earlier may also help reconcile some Low Chronology regnal dates of Khufu to Pepi II cited by Gautschy et al. (2017 Table 4) with the ^{14}C determinations of these kings (Dee 2013).

Also, two papyri from the mortuary temple of King Raneferef provide Wagy (*w3g*) feast dates: A 3rd month [...] day 28, in Document IV, and 1st month of Akhet day 23-29 or 29. These probably can be no earlier than Niuserre year 1 or later than Pepi II (Gautschy et al 2017), but with no certain attribution several models might be possible.

Although the ointment jar date may offer support for the existence of the Sothic cycle in the Old Kingdom, the accuracy of a Sothic date remains a question, since a single significant calendar reform could move a date by decades, if not significantly more.

Bibliography

Ahlstrom, G. W.

1994. *The History of Ancient Palestine.* Minneapolis: Fortress.

Albright, W. F.

1935. Archaeology and the Date of the Hebrew Conquest of Palestine, *BASOR* 58: 10–18.

1947. Reviewed work: *Stüdien over de El-Amarnabrieven en het Oude-Testament inzonderheid uit historisch Oogpunt. JNES* 6(1): 58–59.

1966. *Amarna Letters from Palestine, Syria, the Philistines and Phoenicia.* Cambridge: Cambridge University Press.

Aling, C. F.

1981. *Egypt and Bible History: From Earliest Times to 1000 B.C.* Grand Rapids: Baker Book House.

2002. Joseph in Egypt Part 1. *B&S* 15(1): 21-23.

Aston, D.

2012. Radiocarbon, wine jars and New Kingdom chronology. *AEundL* 22: 289–315.

Battenfield, J. R.

1972. A Consideration of the Identity of the Pharaoh of Genesis 47. *JETS* 15(2): 77–85.

Berman, L. M.

1998. Overview of Amenhotep III and his reign, in D. O'Connor and E. H. Cline (eds.), *Amenhotep III: Perspectives on His Reign.* Ann Arbor: University of Michigan Press: 1–25.

Bierbrier, M. L.

1995. How Old Was Hatshepsut? *GM* 144: 15–19.

Bietak, M.

2006. Nomads or Mnmn.t-shepherds in the Eastern Nile Delta in the New Kingdom. *I Will Speak the Riddles of Ancient Times: Archaeological and Historical Studies in Honor of Amihai Mazar on the Occasion of His Sixtieth Birthday* 1: 123–136.

2010. *Houses, Palaces and Development of Social Structure in Avaris Part I* 60: 11–40. Verlag der Österreichischen Akademie der Wissenschaften.

2015a. On the Historicity of the Exodus: What Egyptology Today Can Contribute to Assessing the Biblical Account of the Sojourn in Egypt, in T. E. Levy, T. Schneider and W. H. C. Propp (eds.), *Israel's Exodus in Transdisciplinary Perspective.* Heidelberg-New York: Springer, Switzerland: 17–36.

2015b. Recent Discussions about the Chronology of the Middle and the Late Bronze Ages in the Eastern Mediterranean: Part I. *BiOr* 72(3): 317–335.

2017. Harbours and Coastal Military Bases in Egypt in the Second Millennium B.C. Avaris, Peru-nefer, Pi-Ramesse, in H. Willems and J. M. Dahms (eds.), *The Nile: Natural and Cultural Landscape in Egypt*. Mainz Historical Cultural Sciences 36, Mainz: 53–70.

2018. The Many Ethnicities in Avaris: Evidence from the Northern Borderland of Egypt, in J. Budka, and J. Auenmüller (eds.), *From Microcosm to Macrocosm: Individual Households and Cities in Ancient Egypt and Nubia*. Leiden: 73–92.

Bietak, M., and Forstner-Müller, I.

2011. The Topography of New Kingdom Avaris and Per-Ramesses, in M. Collier and S. Snape (eds.), *Ramesside Studies in Honour of K.A. Kitchen*. Bolton: 23–51.

Billington, C. E.

2024. The Israelites are the 'Apiru/Habiru in the Amarna Letters. *Artifax* 40(4): 14–16.

Bimson, J. J.

1978. *Redating the Exodus and Conquest*. Sheffield : Department of Biblical Studies, University of Sheffield.

Bolshakov, V. A.

2014. The King's Daughter Neferura: Eventual Heiress of Hatshepsut? *CdE* 89: 248–268.

Brand, P. J.

2020. The Historical Record, in Davies, Vanessa; Laboury, Dimitri (eds.), *The Oxford Handbook of Egyptian Epigraphy and Palaeography*. Oxford Handbooks. Oxford, New York: Oxford University Press.

Breasted, J. H.

1897. Exploration and Discovery. The Israel Tablet. *BW* 9(1): 62–68.

Bright, J.

1972. *A History of Israel*. 2nd ed. London: SCM Press.

Brugsch, H.

1879. *A History of Egypt Under the Pharaohs Derived Entirely from the Monuments*, transl. Henry Danby Seymour, ed. Philip Smith, Vol. 2. London: Murray.

Bryan, B. M.

1991. *The reign of Tuthmosis IV*. Baltimore.

2000. The 18th Dynasty before the Amarna Period (c. 1550-1352 BC), in I. Shaw (ed.), *The Oxford History of Ancient Egypt*. Oxford: Oxford University Press: 218–271.

Caiger, S. L.

1936. *Bible and Spade: An Introduction to Biblical Archaeology*. Oxford University Press.

Clayton, P.

1994. *Chronicle of the Pharaohs: The Reign-by-Reign Record of the Rulers of the Dynasties of Egypt*. London: Thames and Hudson Ltd.

Cline, E. H.

2006. The Early Reign of Thutmose III, in Cline, E. H., and O'Connor, D. (eds.), *Thutmose III: A New Biography*. University of Michigan Press.

Cochavi-Rainey, Z.

2005. *To the King My Lord. Letters from El-Amarna, Kumidi, Taanach and Other Letters from the Fourteenth Century BCE*. Jerusalem: Bialik Institute.

Cogan, M.

2001. *1 Kings*. 10. New York: Doubleday.

Collins, S.

2005. Using Historical Synchronisms to Identify the Pharaoh of the Exodus. *BRB* V(8): 1–70.

Coucke, V.

1928. *Chronologie Biblique*, in *Louis Pirot* (ed.), *Supplément au Dictionnaire de la Bible*. Paris: Librairie Letouzey et Ané.

Curtis, E. L.

1889. Chronology of the Old Testament, in James Hastings (ed.), *A Dictionary of the Bible*. I. Edinburgh: T. & T. Clark.

Day, J.

1995. The Pharaoh of the Exodus, Josephus and Jubilees. *VT* 45(3): 377–378.

Dee, M. W.

2013. A Radiocarbon-based Chronology for the Old Kingdom. *Radiocarbon and the chronologies of ancient Egypt, 209*.

De Pietri, M.

2016. Relationships Between Egypt and Karkemish During the 2nd Millennium BC: A Brief Overview, in *Cultural & Material Contacts in the Ancient Near East. Proceedings of the International Workshop 1-2 December 2014. Torino*: Apice Libri: 9–15.

Derstine, P.

2016. The Start of the Egyptian Lunar Month in Light of Early Eighteenth Dynasty Sothic and Lunar Dates. *GM* 249: 39–57.

Devecci, E., and Miller, J. L.

2011. Hittite-Egyptian Synchronisms and their Consequences for Ancient Near Eastern Chronology, in J. Mynářová (ed.), *Egypt and the Near East-the Crossroads*. Prague: 139–176.

DeVries, S. J.

1985. *1 Kings*. Word Biblical Commentary 12. Word Books.

Dodson, A.

2014. *Amarna sunrise: Egypt from golden age to age of heresy*. Oxford University Press.

Donadoni, S.

1997. *The Egyptians*. University of Chicago Press: Chicago, IL and London.

Eames, C.

2023. The Amarna Letters: Proof of Israel's Invasion of Canaan? *LSS* 2(2): 28–33.

Finegan, J.

1946. *Light from the Ancient Past: The Archaeological Background of the Hebrew-Christian Religion*. Princeton University Press.

1964. *The Handbook of Biblical Chronology*: *Principles of Time Reckoning in the Ancient World and Problems of Chronology in the Bible*. Princeton University Press.

1998. *The Handbook of Biblical Chronology*: *Principles of Time Reckoning in the Ancient World and Problems of Chronology in the Bible*. Revised Edition. Peabody: Hendrickson Publishers.

Fischer, P.

1999. Chocolate-on-White Ware: Typology, Chronology and Provenance: The Evidence from Tell Abu al-Kharaz, Jordan Valley. *BASOR* 313: 1–29.

Garcia, J. L.

2019. A Chronological Perspective on the Transition from Amenhotep III to Amenhotep IV / Akhenaten. *AulaOr* 37(1): 61–89.

Garstang, J.

1934. Jericho: City and Necropolis, Fourth Report. *AAA* 21: 99–136.

1948. *The Story of Jericho*. London: Marshall, Morgan & Scott.

Gautschy, R.

2014. A Reassessment of the Absolute Chronology of the Egyptian New Kingdom and Its 'Brotherly' Countries. *AEundL* 24: 141–158.

2017a. Remarks Concerning the Alleged Solar Eclipse of Muršili II. *AOF* 44(1): 23–29.

Gautschy, R., Habicht, M. E., Galassi, F. M., Rutica, D., Rühli, F. J., and Hannig, R.

2017b. A new astronomically-based chronological model for the Egyptian Old Kingdom. *JEH* 10 (2): 69–108.

Gedge, E. C.

2022. *Chronology of the Kingdom*, Putaruru.

Geoghegan, J. C.

2006. The Time, Place, and Purpose of the Deuteronomistic History: The Evidence of "Until This Day." *BJS* 347. Providence: Brown University.

Ginzel, F. K.

1899. *Spezieller Kanon der Sonnen- und Mondfinsternisse für das Ländergebiet der klassischen Altertumswissenschaften und den Zeitraum von 900 v. Chr. bis 600 nach Chr.* Mayer & Müller.

Gitin, S.

2019. *The Ancient Pottery of Israel and its Neighbors from the Middle Bronze Age Through the Late Bronze Age.* Jerusalem: IES.

Giveon, R.

1969. Tuthmosis IV and Asia. *JNES* 28(1): 54–59.

Green, A. R.

1983. David's Relations with Hiram: Biblical and Josephan Evidence for Tyrian Chronology, in *The Word of the Lord Shall Go Forth: Essays in Honor of David Noel Freedman in Celebration of His Sixtieth Birthday, ed. Carol Meyers and Michael Patrick O'Connor.* Winona Lake, IN: Eisenbrauns.

Gunn, D. M., and Fewell, D. N.

1993. *Narrative in the Hebrew Bible*. Oxford University Press.

Gunneweg, A. H. J.

1989. *Geschichte Israels: von den Anfängen bis Bar Kochba und von Theodor Herzl bis zur Gegenwart,* 2. Kohlhammer.

Habermehl, A.

2013. Revising the Egyptian Chronology: Joseph as Imhotep, and Amenhotep IV as Pharaoh of the Exodus. *ICC* 7(1): 1–33.

Haug, B.

2024. *Garden of Egypt: Irrigation, Society, and the State in the Premodern Fayyūm*. Ann Arbor: University of Michigan Press.

Hayes, J. H., and Hooker, P. K.

2007. *A New Chronology for the Kings of Israel and Judah and Its Implications for Biblical History and Literature*. Westminster John Knox Press.

Hayes, W. C., and Edwards, I. E.

1971. The Middle Kingdom in Egypt. Internal history from the rise of the Heracleopolitans to the death of Ammenemes III, in *The Cambridge Ancient History; Vol. 1, Pt. 2: Early History of the Middle East* 2: 464–531.

Haynes, A. E.

1896. The Date of the Exodus. *PEQ* 28(3): 245–258.

Harris, J. E., and Wente, E. F.

1980. *An X-ray Atlas of the Royal Mummies*. University of Chicago Press.

Helck, W.

1962. *Die Beziehungen Ägyptens zu Vorderasien im 3. und 2. Jahrtausend v. Chr.: 2*. Wiesbaden: Harrassowitz.

1988. Erneut das angebliche Sothis-Datum des Pap. Ebers und die Chronologie der 18. Dynastie. *SAK* 15: 149–164.

Hentschel, K.

2021. Depiction of a Solar Eclipse from 1143 BCE in the Pharaonic Tomb KV9 Near Thebes. *IJHCS* 7(2): 11–23.

Hoeh, H. L.

1983. *Notes Regarding Reigns of Kings*. Ambassador College.

Hoffmeier, J. K.

1996. *Israel in Egypt: The Evidence for the Authenticity of the Exodus Tradition*. Oxford University Press.

2021. The Thirteenth-Century (Late-Date) Exodus View, in M. D. Janzen (ed.), *Five Views on the Exodus: Historicity, Chronology, and Theological Implications*. Grand Rapids: Zondervan.

Hornung, E.

2001. *Akhenaten and the Religion of Light*. Cornell University Press.

Huber, P. J.

2001. The Solar Omen of Muršili II. *JAOS* 121(4): 640–644.

2011. The Astronomical Basis of Egyptian Chronology of the Second Millenium BC. *JEH* 4: 172–227.

Ibrahim, O.

2019. Hydrology of the Great Fayoum Depression till the 12th Dynasty: Archaeological and Philological Evidences of Artificial Water Entry. *MJTHR* Article 2, 8(1): 29–46.

Israelit-Groll, S.

1998. The Egyptian Background of the Exodus and the Crossing of the Reed Sea: A New Reading of Papyrus Anastasi VIII, in I. Shirun-Grumach (ed.), *Jerusalem Studies in Egyptology*, AeAT 40. Wiesbaden: Harrassowitz Verlag: 173–192.

Jack, J. W.

1925. *The Date of the Exodus in the Light of External Evidence*. Edinburgh, T. & T. Clark.

Jansen-Winkeln, K.

2006. Dynasty 21, in Erik Hornung, Rolf Krauss and David A. Warburton (eds.), *Ancient Egyptian Chronology*. Leiden: Brill: 218–233.

Janzen, M.

2023. Making a Case for the Historicity of Moses. *Artifax* 39(3): 20–23.

Kennedy, T.

2011. *The Israelite Conquest: History or Myth?: An Achaeological Evaluation of the Israelite Conquest During the Periods of Joshua and the Judges*. University of South Africa.

2020. *Unearthing the Bible: 101 Archaeological Discoveries that Bring the Bible to Life*. Harvest House Publishers.

2023. The Bronze Age Destruction of Jericho, Archaeology, and the Book of Joshua. *Religions* 14: 796.

Kenyon, K., and Holland, T. A.

1983. *Excavations at Jericho V. The Pottery Phases of the Tell and Other Finds*. Jerusalem: British School of Archaeology.

Kitchen, K. A.

1966. *Ancient Orient and Old Testament*. London: Inter-Varsity Press.

1996. The Historical Chronology of Ancient Egypt: A Current Assessment. *AcAr* 67: 1–13.

2003. *On the Reliability of the Old Testament*. Wm. B. Eerdmans.

Knudtzon, J. A., Weber, O., and Ebeling, E.

1915. *Die El-Amarna-Tafeln, mit Einleitung und Erläuterungen*. J. C. Hinrichs' Sche Buchhandlung. Leipzig.

Kraemer, B.

2010. The Meandering Identity of a Fayum Canal: The Henet of Moeris/Dioryx Kleonos/Bahr Wardan/Abdul Wahbi. In *The Proceedings of the 25th International Congress of Papyrology* 25(1). MPublishing, University of Michigan Library.

Krauss, R.

1985. *Sothis and Moon data. Studies on astronomical and technical chronology of ancient Egypt* (*Egyptological contributions* from *Hildesheim.* 20). Barstenberg, Hildesheim.

2005. Das wrŝ-Datum aus Jahr 5 von Shoshenq [I]. *DE* 62: 43–48.

2007. Die Mahler-Borchardtsche These über die Apis-Inthronisationen bei Vollmond. *APA* 39: 339–348.

Krauss, R., and Warburton, D. A.

2006. Conclusions and a Postscript to Part II, Chapter I, in Erik Hornung, Rolf Krauss and David A. Warburton (eds.), *Ancient Egyptian Chronology*. Leiden: Brill: 473–489.

Laboury, D.

2014. How and Why Did Hatshepsut Invent the Image of Her Royal Power? in J. M. Galán, B. M. Bryan, and P. F. Dorman (eds.), *Creativity and Innovation in the Reign of Hatshepsut*. Oriental Institute of the University of Chicago.

Larsson, P. O., and Larsson, L. A.

2020. Towards an Absolute Scientific Date for the Egyptian New Kingdom, Part 2: The New Moon Dates: 1–17.

Lepsius, R.

1849. *Die Chronologie Der Aegypter*. Berlin: Nicolaische Buchhandlung.

1852. *Briefe aus Aegypten, Aethiopien und der Halbinsel des Sinai geschrieben in den Jahren 1842-1845*. Verlag von Wilhelm Hertz: Bessersche Buchhandlung.

Letellier, B.

1979. La cour à péristyle de Thoutmosis IV à Karnak. *B SFE* 84 (1979): 52–71.

Luft, U.

1992. Remarks of a Philologist on Egyptian Chronology. *AEundL* 3: 109–114.

Mahler, E.

1890. Ramses II. 1348 – 1281 vor Chr. Geb: Auszug aus einem Schreiben. *ZÄS* 28(1-2): 32–34.

1896. *Der Pharao des Exodus*. Moriz Waizner & Sohn.

1901. Art. II.–The Exodus. *JRAS* 33(1): 33–67.

Martín-Valentín, F. J., and Bedman, T.

2017. Chapel of the tomb belonging to Amenhotep III's Vizier, Amenhotep Huy. Asasif Tomb No. 28, Luxor-West Bank. Excavation results: 'Vizier Amenhotep Huy Project' (2009-2014), in *Proceedings of the XI International Congress of Egyptologists, Florence, Italy 23-30 August 2015*. Archaeopress Publishing Ltd.

Matić, U.

2016. (De)Queering Hatshepsut: Binary Bind in Archaeology of Egypt and Kingship Beyond the Corporeal. *JAMT* 23(3): 810–831.

McFall, L.

2010. The Chronology of Saul and David. *JETS* 53: 475–533.

Melandri, I.

2011. Nuove considerazioni su una statua da Qaw El-Kebir al Museo delle Antichità Egizie di Torino. Vicino & Medio Oriente XV: 249–270.

Mercator, G.

1569. *Chronologia: Hoc est, temporvm demonstratio exactissima, ab initio mvndi, vsqve ad annvm Domini M. D. LXVIII.* Cologne: Birckmann.

Merrill, E. H.

1994. *Deuteronomy*. 4, The New American Commentary. Nashville: Broadman & Holman Publishers.

Meyer, E.

1904. *Aegyptische chronologie 1*. Verlag der Königl. Akademie der Wissenschaften.

Mieroop, M.

2011. *A History of Ancient Egypt*. West Sussex: Wiley-Blackwell.

Miller, J. L.

2007. Amarna Age chronology and the identity of Nibhururiya in the light of a newly reconstructed Hittite text. *AOF* 34(2): 252–293.

2008. The Rebellion of Hatti's Syrian Vassals and Egypt's Meddling in Amurru, in A. Archi, and R. Francia (eds.), *VI Congresso Internazionale di Ittitologia, Roma, 5–9 settembre 2005*. Roma: "L'Erma" di Bretschneider: 533–554.

Moore, J.

2023. The Biblical Conquest: Myth or History? *B&S* 36(3): 10–21.

Moran, W. L.

1992. *The Amarna Letters*. Baltimore: Johns Hopkins University Press.

Morgan, J. R.

2023. *The Snares of Thoth: A Social History of Provincial Administration in Ptolemaic Egypt*. Yale University.

Morgan, L.

2004. Feline Hunters in the Tell el-Dab'a Paintings: Iconography and Dating. *AEundL* 14: 285–298.

Morkot, R. G.

2010. *The A to Z of ancient Egyptian warfare*. 196. Rowman & Littlefield.

Muller, P. M., and Stephenson, F. R.

1975. The Accelerations of the Earth and Moon from Early Astronomical Observations, in G. D. Rosenberg and S. K. Runcorn (eds.), *Growth Rhythms and The History of Earth's Rotation*. New York: 459–533.

Mynářová, J.

2011. Expressions of Dates and Time in the Amarna Letters. *AEundL* 21: 123–128.

Na'aman, N.

1975. *The Political Disposition and Historical Development of Eretz Israel according to the Amarna Letters* (Ph.D. Dissertation). Tel Aviv University.

Nadig, P.

2016. *Hatszepsut*. Prószyński i S-ka.

Nigro, L.

2020. The Italian-Palestinian expedition to Tell es-Sultan, ancient Jericho (1997–2015): Archaeology and valorisation of material and immaterial heritage. *Digging up Jericho: Past, present and future*. Oxford: Archaeopress Publishing Ltd: 175–214.

2021. *Tell es-Sultan/Jericho in the Iron Age*. (Conference Presentation). 2021 ASOR Annual Meeting Virtual Component. December 12, 2021.

2023. Tell es-Sultan/Jericho in the Late Bronze Age. An overall reconstruction in the light of most recent research. *Durch die Zeiten. Through the ages. Festschrift für Dieter Vieweger Aufsätze zu Ehren von Dieter Vieweger*: 599–614.

Niwiński, A.

1979. Problems in the Chronology and Genealogy of the XXIst Dynasty: New Proposals for their Interpretation. *JARCE* 16: 49–68.

O'Connor, D.

2006. An Enigmatic Pharaoh, in Cline, E. H., and O'Connor, D. (eds.), *Thutmose III: A New Biography*. University of Michigan Press.

Osgood, A. J. M.

1984. The times of the Judges—a chronology. *JoC* 1: 141–148.

Parker, R.

1950. The Calendars of Ancient Egypt. *SAOC* 26: 9–23.

1957. The Lunar Dates of Thutmose III and Ramesses II. *JNES* 16(1): 39–43.

1970. The beginning of the lunar month in ancient Egypt. *JNES* 29(4): 217–220.

Pawlicki, F., Yacoub, G., El Tayeb, M., and Gaafar, N.

2007. Princess Neferure in the Temple of Queen Hatshepsut at Deir el-Bahari. Failed Heiress to the Pharaoh's Throne? *Et* 21: 110–127.

2017. *The Main Sanctuary of Amun-Re in the Temple of Hatshepsut at Deir el-Bahari*. Polish Centre of Mediterranean Archaeology, University of Warsaw.

Payne, J. B.

1954. *An Outline of Hebrew History*. Grand Rapids: Baker Book House.

Peterson, B. N.

2015. *The Authors of the Deuteronomistic History: Locating a Tradition in Ancient Israel*. Minneapolis: Fortress.

Petrie, W. F.

1896. The Date of the Exodus. *PEQ* 28(4): 335–337.

Petrovich, D.

2006. Amenhotep II and the Historicity of the Exodus-Pharaoh. *TMSJ* 17(1): 81–110.

2013. Toward Pinpointing the Timing of the Egyptian Abandonment of Avaris during the Middle of the 18th Dynasty. *JAEI* 5(2): 9–28.

2019. Determining the Precise Length of the Israelite Sojourn in Egypt. *NEAS Bulletin* 64: 21–41.

2021. *Origins of the Hebrews: New Evidence of Israelites in Egypt from Joseph to the Exodus*. Nashville: New Creation.

Piccione, P. A.

2003. The Women of Thutmose III in the Stelae of the Egyptian Museum. *JSSEA* 30: 91–102.

Rainey, A. F.

2015. The Tell-el-Amarna Letters: Transcription and Translation, in William Schniedewind and Zipora Cochavi-Rainey (eds.), *The El-Amarna Correspondence: A New*

Edition of the Cuneiform Letters from the Site of El-Amarna based on Collation of all Extant Tablets, Volume 1. Leiden: Brill: 57–1267.

Raspe, L.

1998. Manetho on the Exodus: A Reappraisal. *JSQ* 5(2): 124–155.

Ratié, S.

1972. *La reine-pharaon*. Julliard.

Rea, J.

1961. The Time of the Oppression and the Exodus. *GTJ* 2(1): 5–14.

Roaf, M.

2012. The Fall of Babylon in 1499 NC or 1595 MC. *Akkadica* 133(2): 147–174.

Rowley, H. H.

1950. *From Joseph to Joshua*. London: British Academy.

Shaw, I., and Nicholson, P.

1995. *Dictionary of Ancient Egypt*. London: The British Museum Press.

Shea, W. H.

1979. Exodus, Date of. *The International Standard Bible Encyclopedia*. 2. Grand Rapids: 230–238.

2003. Amenhotep II as Pharaoh of the Exodus. *B&S* 16: 41–51.

Sandars, N. K.

1985. *The Sea peoples Warriors of the ancient Mediterranean*. Revised Edition. Thames and Hudson, London.

Sellin, E., and Watzinger, C.

1913. *Jericho: Die Ergebnissi der Ausgrabungen*. Leipzig: J. C. Hinrichs.

Smith Jr., H. B.

2024. 1 Kings 6:1 and the Date of the Exodus from the Masoretic and Septuagint Textual Traditions. *NEAS Bulletin* 69: 41–64.

Spalinger, G. M.

2018. Feasts and Fights: Essays on Time in Ancient Egypt. *YES* 10. New Haven.

Steinmann, A. E.

2011. *From Abraham to Paul: A Biblical Chronology*. Saint Louis: Concordia.

Stripling, S.

2021. The Fifteenth-Century (Early-Date) Exodus View, in M. D. Janzen (ed.), *Five Views on the Exodus: Historicity, Chronology, and Theological Implications*. Grand Rapids: Zondervan.

Stripling, S., Galil, G., Kumpova, I. et al.

2023. You are Cursed by the God YHW: an early Hebrew inscription from Mt. Ebal. *Herit Sci* 11(1) 105: 1–24.

Tetley, M. C., and Tetley, B.

2014. *The Reconstructed Chronology of the Egyptian Kings*. Barry W. Tetley.

Thiele, E. R.

1944. The chronology of the kings of Judah and Israel. *JNES* 3(3): 137–186.

Tompsett, D.

2023. *Ancient Israel in Egypt: Through a Glass, Darkly*. Eugene: Wipf & Stock.

Tyldesley, J.

1996. *Hatchepsut: The Female Pharaoh*. N.Y.: Viking.

von Beckerath, J.

1994. *Chronologie des ägyptischen Neuen Reiches.* (Hildesheimer ägyptologische Beiträge 39). Hildesheim: Gerstenberg.

Weinstein, J. M.

1998. Egypt and the Levant in the Reign of Amenhotep III, in D. O'Connor and E. H. Cline (eds.), *Amenhotep III: Perspectives on His Reign.* Ann Arbor: 223–235.

Wente, E. F.

1967. On the Chronology of the Twenty-First Dynasty. *JNES* 26(3): 155–176.

1975. Thutmose III Accession and the Beginning of the New Kingdom. *JNES* 34(4): 265–272.

1995. Who Was Who Among the Royal Mummies. *The OINN* 144: 1–6.

Wendrich, W., and Holdaway, S. J.

2017. Landscape archaeology of the Desert Fayum, in *The Desert Fayum reinvestigated: The Early to Mid-Holocene landscape archaeology of the Fayum North Shore, Egypt.* Los Angeles, CA: The Cotsen Institute of Archaeology Press: 1–7.

Wente, E. F., and Van Siclen III, C. C.

1976. A Chronology of the New Kingdom, in: J. H. Johnson and E. F. Wente (eds.), *Studies in Honor of George R. Hughes. SAOC* 39, Chicago: 217–261.

Whiston, W., and Tooke, B.

1702. *A Short View of the Chronology of the Old Testament, and of the Harmony of the Four Evangelists.* Cambridge: Cambridge University Press.

Wilhelm, G., and Boese, J.

1987. Absolute Chronologie und die hethitische Geschichte des 15. und 14. Jharhunderts v. Chr, in P. Astrom, (ed.), *High, Middle or Low?* Gothenburg: 74–117.

Wilkinson, J.G.,

1878. *The Manners and Customs of the Ancient Egyptians.* 2. London: John Murray.

Windle, B.

2025a. *Tell es-Sultan/Jericho City V: The City the Israelites Conquered?* M.A. thesis, Trinity Southwest University.

2025b. Letters from the Biblical World: The Amarna Letters. *Bible Archaeology Report.* August 1, 2025.

Wood, B. G.

1997. The Role of Shechem in the Conquest of Canaan, in *To Understand the Scriptures: Essays in Honor of William*

H. Shea, ed. David Merling. Berrien Springs, MI: Institute of Archaeology: 245–256.

2003. From Ramesses to Shiloh: Archaeological Discoveries Bearing on the Exodus-Judges Period, in David M. Howard Jr. and Michael A. Grisanti (eds.), *Giving the Sense. Understanding and Using Old Testament Historical Texts*. Leicester: Apollos: 256–282.

2005. The Rise and Fall of the 13th-century Exodus-Conquest Theory. *JETS* 48(3): 475–489.

2007. The Biblical Date for the Exodus Is 1446 BC: A Response to James Hoffmeier. *JETS* 50(2): 249–258.

2008a. Recent Research on the Date and Setting of the Exodus. *B&S* 21(4): 97–108.

2008b. A Critical Analysis of the Evidence from Ralph Hawkins for a Late-Date Exodus-Conquest. *JETS* 51(2): 225–243.

Wood, L.

1970. *A Survey of Israel's History*. Zondervan.

Young, E.

1963. Some Notes on the Chronology and Genealogy of the Twenty-First Dynasty. *JARCE* 2: 99–112.

Young, R. C.

2003. When Did Solomon Die? *JETS* 46(4): 589–603.

www.ingramcontent.com/pod-product-compliance
Lightning Source LLC
Chambersburg PA
CBHW040845120626
46547CB00001B/32